A SPADE AMONG
THE RUSHES

A SPADE AMONG THE RUSHES

MARGARET LEIGH

ORIGIN

This edition published in 2018 by
Birlinn Origin, an imprint of
Birlinn Limited
West Newington House
10 Newington Road
Edinburgh
EH9 1QS

www.birlinn.co.uk

First published by Birlinn Limited in 2011

ISBN: 978 1 91247 616 9
eBook ISBN: 978 0 85790 975 6

British Library Cataloguing-in-Publication Data
A catalogue record for this book is available
from the British Library

Typeset by Geethik Technologies, India
Printed and bound by Clays Ltd, Elcograf S.p.A.

CONTENTS

1	I find Smirisary	*page*	1
2	I Become a Crofter in Smirisary		4
3	I Settle In		11
4	Fire, Water and Bread		22
5	Byre and Barn		34
6	The Garden and the Blaran Boidheach		41
7	The Lon and the Blar Eorna		55
8	Winter Nights		63
9	Spring Work		74
10	Blossom		85
11	Lovely May		96
12	Cows		105
13	Amenities		115
14	Fences and Drains		123
15	The "Star of Smirisary"		130
16	Birth and Death		138
17	The Land Court Visits Smirisary		144
18	Haymaking		151
19	The Great August Drought		157
20	Autumn Days		167

[continued overleaf

CONTENTS CONTINUED

21 The Highland Problem   *page* 177

22 The Amateur Crofter   184

23 Conclusion   189

A Map of Smirisary, pp. viii & ix

Foreword

My father and I crofted in Smirisary at the same time as Margaret Leigh became a crofter in the 1940s. At that time there were four families working the land; they were hard but happy days. Many an hour I spent with Margaret, exchanging stories while herding cattle.

Margaret Leigh was the only crofter in Smirisary with a horse. To the great amusement of the older folk it would not always do as she wanted it to. However, it was a great help to us all when peat had to be brought home.

Margaret very quickly became part of the crofting community and was well thought of. It all seems such a long time ago!

I am 81 years old; I have seen many changes, not least of which is the end of the crofting community as I knew it.

Katy Maclean *née* Gillies
Gortean
Smirisary
1996

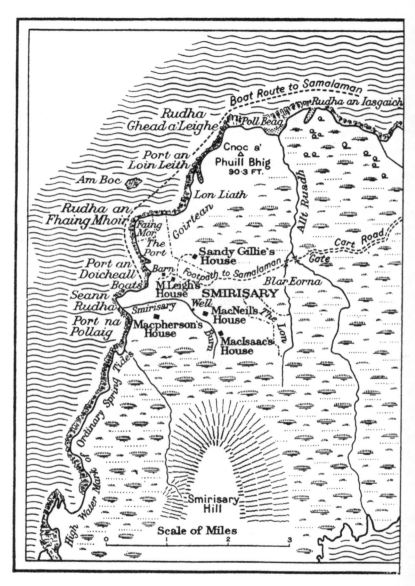

A MAP OF

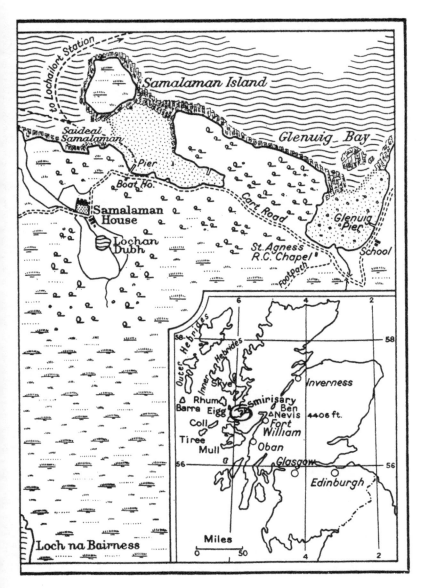

SMIRISARY

I Find Smirisary

IT was in March 1940, that I first set eyes upon Smirisary. My friend Graham Croll had seen it before and told me to be sure to go there as it was the very place that would appeal to me. He was right. I had been too long imprisoned in glens, where leaning hills frowned down on me and took away the winter sun. But Smirisary – the queer name, half Norse, half Gaelic, means "butter shieling" – lay open to the western ocean, and its green crofting land, enamelled with flowers, shone like a jewel, half-ringed by hills of rock and heather. There were boats drawn up on the shore and a few houses with byres and barns scattered round the edge of the arable, all stone and nearly all thatched: enough to banish loneliness without destroying privacy. And in the midst a burn, sliding between its deeply eroded banks, too small to raise its voice against the sea. The township of five households was sheltered from the east by high braes, always steep, in places sheer, with tracks leading to more arable above and the great world beyond. There were men herding cows in little groups or vanishing over the pass with creels to the distant peat moss. Upon the burden of the surf was thrown the pattern of other sounds – a collie barking, a cock crowing, the brush of wind in withered bent and heather, the grinding of keel on shingle. Thus I found Smirisary, and even on that raw March day of wind and chilly showers, I fell in love with it. And having now lived there for four years and seen it at all seasons and in every kind of weather; and having done and suffered all sorts of things in it – pleasant, laborious, ridiculous, incredible, but never for a moment boring – I find myself more in love with it than ever.

Slithering down the precipitous footpath, I passed the

back of the house in which I now live. The walls were of solid, squared stone, excellently wrought, the work of a mason building for himself. But the place had stood empty for twelve years, and the galvanised iron roof was perishing for lack of paint and gaping at the ridge, so that rain seeped down upon the rotting boards of the floor. Nothing had been removed from the interior; the door was intact and bolted, the window panes unbroken, the partitions standing. Pressing my nose against the dusty glass, I could see that there were two large rooms and one small one. It came to me that the house, if repaired, would make an attractive home; but so have I said of a dozen derelict cottages seen in my wanderings, and I thought no more about it. The thing that impressed me most was a pillar of dressed stone, surmounted by a pyramid of the same material, on which a gate had once hung. The gate was gone, and the pillar leaned at a rakish and dangerous angle in a wilderness of nettles; but it gave to the house an exotic distinction it has never quite lost. I passed through a little field full of rushes and the rustling ghosts of last year's thistles and burdocks, and across the burn to Annie Macpherson's house where Graham had told me to call. She stood at the door, a thin upright figure, watching the stranger approach, and Angus and her brother lingered on the byre path, also at gaze. I greeted him, and he replied in the formal careful English of a habitual Gaelic speaker. Little did I think that in three years' time we should be chattering in the old language as we spread dung or turned hay.

I was sufficiently interested in Smirisary to write to the owner of the estate, asking to whom the empty house belonged. But I heard no more, and it appeared afterwards that he had never received my letter. An enquiry sent elsewhere went also unanswered: the house was clearly not for me, and I let the matter drop. In any case I was deep in war-time farm work in Ross-shire and the monstrous threat of that summer made the Smirisary plan – if plan it could be called – seem only one more of the impossible, visionary things we were going to do or have "after the war". The remote Highlands were buzzing with every kind of scare – about invasion, about parachute landings, about the billeting of evacuees and of soldiers. At Fernaig, our energies were bent on food production and we thought of little else.

In December 1940, when my services on the farm were for the moment not required, I went to Barra for several weeks and wrote the greater part of *Driftwood and Tangle*. I had a furnished cottage, in which I lived with only a dog for company. Later, when I had returned to Fernaig for the spring work, I heard that the cottage was for sale, and nearly bought it, though it had not a square yard of land. Then news came in letters about mysterious "works" within a mile of the place, on which most of the population were employed. "An aerodrome", I thought, and withdrew my offer. The flat *machairs* of the Hebrides are particularly suitable for runways, and my thoughts turned again to rocky Smirisary where there is no level ground. The "works" proved to be only a radio-location station; but in most ways I was not sorry that the plan had fallen through. Houses and land are scarce in the Outer Islands and should not be appropriated by strangers. It is better to seek a derelict place which nobody wants and put it in order. This, in theory, should arouse no jealousy or resentment, although in practice you may find yourself unpopular, like the man who wins a race with a supposedly dud horse he has picked up cheap.

I Become a Crofter in Smirisary

IN December 1941, I was staying with Graham Croll and his mother at their farm in Morvern. From time to time we talked of Smirisary but a far more ambitious scheme had begun to ferment in our minds. It appeared that the Glenuig estate might be for sale; if so, Mrs Croll might buy it, and I would take the croft in Smirisary and we should all be together. Each evening we talked and planned for hours. There was a six-inch Ordnance map hanging over Graham's desk and we would clamber up in turn, or even both together, gazing and measuring and discussing. Finally in January, Graham went to Edinburgh to see the proprietor, in no way deterred by hearing that the old gentleman was ill in bed. By this time I had decided to take the croft, whether Mrs Croll bought Glenuig or not, and so I asked Graham to find out about this also. Negotiations for the estate were bound to be slow – actually they lasted nine months – but house and croft had been derelict for twelve years, and could be had for the asking. So in the February following, my name was entered on the Land Court's Register at Fort William and I became an official landholder. This was nearly two years after I had first looked upon the croft.

The reader may here ask, as most of my friends have done, why I wanted a croft at all. The question is a fair one and I will try to answer it as best I can. When at Michaelmas 1938 I left Newton – the "Trenoweth" of *Harvest of the Moor* – it was with the resolve to take no more active part in farming. The farm had been reasonably successful; indeed, at one time, I even toyed with the idea of buying and improving it. But a steady review of the facts dissuaded me. I was past forty and not nearly as strong as some of my activities might suggest. My only near relative was a mother over seventy, so that I could not hope to run a family farm. In the previous year, Peter, who had been with me since the first days at Achnadarroch, left to read for a degree in Agriculture, and for labour I had to choose between the expensive and scarce hired man and a succession of more or less inexperienced "mud-students". The future promised nothing but a peck of worries, with the farm management, housekeeping, and most of the outdoor work falling on my shoulders. On the other hand, *Highland Homespun* and *Harvest of the Moor* had been well received and I had as much journalistic work as I could manage. Editors were beginning to commission articles and my publishers were asking for another book. I had always my mother's home in Scotland to fall back upon and it seemed foolish to persist in a job which offered so little time for literature. Yet it cost me a pang to cut myself off from agriculture, without which there would have been no books. For the few things I wrote before I went on the land were anaemic and lacking in originality.

After the sale at Newton, I went to Scotland on horseback, and the course of that journey is described in *My Kingdom for a Horse*. The next few weeks were spent in Kerry, writing up the diaries of the ride. This work went much against the grain. The ride was over and I had lost interest in it. Also the daily labour of composition – for I was never a fluent writer – kept coming between me and the new things I wanted to see and hear. Indeed, I am surprised that *My Kingdom* is no worse a book than it is. For I started tired on that ride, tired to death in body and mind, and the journey, without adventure or suffering, had no lack of petty worries. I might also add the deadening influence of my companion, whom I disappointed by not being the kind of woman my books had led him to expect. This nuisance, which I suppose must afflict other writers, has dogged me incessantly.

Then, for the second time in my blasted generation, came war crashing in upon my literary schemes, as in 1914 it had broken the young ambitions of an Oxford student. Only this time I was mature and had gained some measure of wisdom and acquiescence. Literature, at least of the minor sort that can flourish only in a stable society, withered into silence or girded itself for propaganda. I returned to farming, no longer on my own account, but as assistant to the Laird, who had no one on the place but an elderly shepherd. I enjoyed the work and the company of friends but was always haunted by an unappeasable longing for independence, and it occurred to me that I might take a small croft with a cottage that would house me in winter, for on a Highland farm there is little to do in the darkest months. And, after the war, I could live there all the year round at very small cost, producing most of my own food. At that time it seemed likely that the war would be prolonged until general exhaustion and impoverishment forced a halt; and then farewell to any hope of earning money with my pen – a spade would serve me better.

On a croft, life could be reduced to the barest necessities without loss of dignity or freedom; and now that the crofting community has become the darling of Government and public alike, crofters get many advantages at very small expense. Frugality is natural in Scotland and you lose no face by it, though English blood is a handicap for the Highlander still believes that an Englishman's pockets are full of gold. If you do not keep a car or a servant, it is not because you cannot afford it, but because you are a crank or a miser. From the worldly point of view I need not perhaps have gone to such extremes. For with an Oxford honours degree and my experience at Reading University, I might have secured some well-paid job before demobilisation closed the door on middle-aged enterprise. But twenty years of country life makes many a breach in the academic facade, and freedom has ever been the breath of my life. I would rather live on potatoes in a one-roomed shack and be my own mistress, than earn a thousand a year and own a master. Foolish as it is – for after all there is freedom wherever the spirit is free – the thought that I must, if alive and fit, do a certain thing at a certain time, in accordance with orders from someone else, makes me sick. Yet as my own employer, I can work sixteen hours a day without a murmur, and at Newton I often did so.

It was not possible for me to visit Smirisary at that time, for the spring work at Fernaig was in full swing. There had also been a tightening up of permit restrictions, by which Lochalsh and Moidart became separate areas, so that travelling between them was very difficult. But Graham, whose farm in Morvern lay within a long day's walk of Glenuig, went over once or twice and, after consulting with Jimmy the young carpenter, reported to me on the necessary minimum of repairs. Jimmy made out specifications for material, which I ordered from the Department of Agriculture.*

In the middle of May I got a few days' holiday, and went down to Glenuig. To my surprise the Laird, Mr Mackintosh, asked me to stay at the Big House. We had never met before, but he was a reader of my books, and that seemed a sufficient introduction. The late winter and spring of 1942 had been excessively dry; heath fires had raged uncontrolled and in many places the hill was black to the sea's edge. But wherever the fires had been stayed, the ground was carpeted with bluebells, primroses, and marsh marigolds; and having seen Smirisary only in the dun deadness of March, I was enchanted. The material had not yet arrived, which was a pity, for I had hoped to get the roof on before the weather broke. However, I went over the house with Jimmy and the details of the work were decided upon. The war cramped our style; timber was scarce and dear, and slates unprocurable.

Then I began to cut peats for the winter. The best banks at Smirisary were far away on the hill, in places remote and inaccessible. Carrying a full creel of peats on my back,

---

* Material for repairs to croft houses and buildings are supplied to bona fide crofters at a cheap rate, carriage paid.

even for a short distance, completely defeats me, and it was essential to get a bank that could be reached with a pony. So I was given a stance at the south-western corner of a big flat called the Laran Mor, about three-quarters of a mile from my house. I borrowed a peat-knife from a neighbour who had finished with it and every morning cut and spread busily, returning to the Big House for lunch. Sometimes I went back in the afternoon also.

The Laran Mor is a lonely spot, remote from the usual tracks. Yet many people came to see how I was getting on, though with Highland tact ostensibly bent upon some other business. I have since come to dislike the Laran Mor, because of its spongy surface and the wide drains that have to be leaped over with a bag of peats on one's back or waded through with leaky Wellingtons. But now the long drought had dried it up and it was not without charm; a perfectly flat expanse of several acres, once drained and cultivated by a laird who cared for farming, but now, after a long twilight of neglect, gone back to moss and rushes. For of all soils, the black peat is the hardest to subdue and the first to return to the wild. Encircled by hills and knollies of heather and rock, it might have been miles inland, except that on days of heavy north-westerly swell you could hear the sea. The sky was full of larks and their song recalled, not without sadness, the cutting of peat on Bodmin Moor, which was also the first job that Peter and I did at Newton. The ancient, satisfying pleasure of laying up stores for the winter came to me again, but now more subdued because I was alone, and a pleasure unshared is halved. I had to leave before the peat was ready to lift but Alan, the neighbour who had lent me the peat-knife, undertook to stack it when fit, and a fine job he made of it.

There were also lighter moments, when Mr Mackintosh took me fishing on Loch na Bairness, a large fresh-water loch high up in the hills; and we rowed among islets thick with trees, in startling contrast with the shores where browsing deer had kept down the vegetation. He was a good fisher-

8

man and, what is more, an excellent cleaner of boots; and this may have been the only occasion on which a laird cleaned a crofter's shoes. Here too I first met Maisie Bright, who was to be a good friend to me.

In July, when I was busy with the hay at Fernaig, I heard that the last of the material had arrived: as Jimmy wittily remarked, it was coming in penny numbers. Every so often I had to sign a receipt for a sack of cement or a bundle of planks or a bag of nails, guided by faith alone, since I could only assume that the goods specified had reached Lochailort Station. But in spite of appalling rain, or perhaps because of it since Jimmy had a croft to work when weather permitted, the house was finished in August, a fortnight before schedule. It was vexatious not to be there in person and, as it turned out, my absence cost me dear. But I did not wish to leave the farm in the middle of the hay-making.

I have always loved pioneering. To make a thing from the beginning is far better than to take it over ready-made. Above all things I would have liked to carve a farm out of an uninhabited island, and that before Ronald Lockley and Fraser Darling had set a fashion in these things. But realism and common sense quickly disposed of this dream. A woman no longer young, too weak to lift a hundredweight bag or crank a marine engine, without husband or brothers or male friends to help, I must be content with a very small achievement. To repair a mined cottage, to make a garden, and bring into cultivation a croft that would support a cow and a pony was all that I could hope to do single-handed. With good land already in cultivation and more conveniences, I could have achieved far more per working hour and I have often been asked why I did not take a better holding. Some years ago I might have thought of it. But now, being alone and with just enough to live on, I do not feel justified in occupying land that might support a family. Nor do I wish to stir up the deep-seated resentment – unreasonable enough in a monogamous community with surplus women running into millions – against spinsters who do or have anything on their own account. However small and poor the croft, I have at least the satisfaction that no one else wants it and, far more than that, I can grow most of my own food, supply my neighbours with winter milk and vegetables and leave one small corner of the Highlands a little better than I found it.

3

I Settle In

IN the third week of October, the season's work at Fernaig ended with the potato-lifting and I was free to leave for Smirisary. At Fort William I met Maisie Bright, who had asked me to stay with her at Glenuig till my own house was ready to live in. We had lunch at the Lochailort hotel and then walked down to the crumbling, slippery little pier from which, at no specific time but just when everything was ready, the store-boat would leave for Glenuig. The pier was a long mile's walk from the station.

Transport, whether in plan or execution, seemed to be our main activity, as it was certainly our favourite topic of conversation. So I had better explain how the inhabitant of Smirisary, his goods, his livestock, and his visitors got from the road and railway at Lochailort to what must have been one of the remotest inhabited places in Britain. In the old days, the journey, if strenuous, was simple. You travelled all the way in your own rowing or sailing boat or, if the weather was unsuitable, you walked. There was no shop nearer than Kinlochmoidart, eight miles distant, and no public service but the post, which was carried on horseback.

When the war began, there was a daily pony post for letters and parcels, and a local motor-boat which went up to Lochailort once a week for heavy goods and passengers. Later, when military camps were established in the district, the boat (weather permitting) ran every day and carried the mails. After the war, it ran only three days a week and, on the alternate days, letters but not parcels were carried by a postman who went on foot.

The store-boat was a solid, beamy little craft, seaworthy and serviceable, but her engine was getting old and no

11

longer very sure. Neither oars nor sail were carried and, in case of a prolonged breakdown, there was nothing for it but to go ashore in the dinghy. In any case, the store-boat went no farther than Glenuig, two miles on the near side of Smirisary, or, if specially chartered, to the private pier at Samalaman which lay between the two. From here to Smirisary, rowing boats must be employed; and in these there was an awful uncertainty for they were dependent on the vagaries of wind, weather, and tides, and on the moods and occupations of their owners. The alternative was a bridle-path impassable for wheels except in one or two places near a big house and, at its worst, bad enough even for a saddle or pack horse. But rough as it was, it prevented Glenuig and Smirisary from being what they almost were – island townships.

To return to ourselves. The only other passenger was the priest. Though the people of Glenuig were Catholic almost to a man, there was in ordinary times no resident priest; the church was served once in three weeks from Mingarry. But, for the sake of Catholic soldiers in the camps, a priest had been stationed at Glenuig, so that those who once heard Mass only every three or four weeks, then heard it every day. Such were the strange results of war.

To me there was something pleasantly familiar in Father Bradley's dark aquiline face, and I was not surprised to learn that he was born in West Cornwall. There was a tang of salt water about him, and his oilskins, long boots, and a scar that might have been made with a cutlass gave him a nautical, even a piratical, appearance, as though he had been private chaplain to a buccaneer. He was sitting in the boat with a gun across his knees and as we went down the loch he took an occasional shot at cormorant or duck, the store-boys steering to suit the chase. It was a calm, beautiful day and we chugged placidly through the narrow channels, threading our way among skerries with the tide-rip chattering against the bows. But when we left Roshven and were well out in the open Minch, a long swell came in from the

west and set the boat rolling. Beyond the green flat of For-
saidh where a filmy waterfall descends the face of the rock,
we came to a point where the huge boulders are rounded
and polished by the ceaseless working of the swell.

At that moment, the priest spied a long, thick plank
rising and falling in the seas. Much timber was coming
ashore in those days, especially on the opposite coast of
Arisaig, which lay exposed to the south-west, and one bay
over there was said to be as full of logs and planks as a
timber-merchant's yard. The engine was stopped and the
boat brought alongside the plank, which must have been
about sixteen feet long, and heavy. As the priest and the
two young men hung over the side to haul it on board,
Maisie and I watched the swell climbing and heaving upon
those polished rocks and subsiding with a hiss, so silken
soft and yet appalling in its latent power. Only a day as
calm as that would have suffered us to drift so near, with
engine stopped and three men hanging over the gunwale.
A few minutes later we opened up Glenuig bay.

Seen from the sea, the whole place could be taken in at
a glance, it was so small. A glen in miniature, with a burn
in the midst, a few scattered crofts, with rigs of corn and
potatoes and hay, all turned by hand and scarcely bigger
than gardens. By the rough boulder pier was the store and
the school and, a little apart on a knoll of trees, the church.
You might see a cow or two, some goats and hens, perhaps
a man herding; only at church-time and on "Ration Day"
was there much traffic, and that all on foot for there was no
vehicle but the estate cart. Far from the turmoil of sword
and speech, Glenuig kept in its heart not only the peace of
all wild places, but the quietness that comes from settled
lives and simple faith, where men are still cradled in a great
tradition now almost gone from a blasted world.

When I say that it is this quietness, this remoteness from
a society corrupted by power and maddened with greed
and fear, that gives to places like Glenuig their unique
beauty, the inhabitants, many of whom have spent their

youth working in cities, may smile at this as a pose, a mere literary affectation on the part of someone who can afford to come for a little while and go again when wearied. Or they may be angry, as if I were suggesting that they were mere bumpkins, though it was shepherds who first saw the star. I have heard people say, "What do you see in this place that is beautiful? We think it ugly!" Yet I am certain that when these same people, after long absence in Glasgow or London or on the high seas, come chugging home in the store-boat or, having missed it, walk the rocky miles by Alisary and Roshven, they will be glad that Glenuig is not quite like other places. They may not admit it; one does not kiss and tell. But there it is.

I found that Father Bradley was living in Maisie's house until a cottage could be made ready for his use. This housing of a priest greatly intrigued her Protestant relations, who doubtless feared the thin end of the Roman wedge. But, as she said, they need not bother themselves; the priest was good company and a great help in housekeeping, since he shared with her the food and coal so freely offered by the faithful. He would light the fire before he went out to say Mass and was always ready to wash dishes or fry us the fish he caught. Being qualified in medicine, he would attend the sick – a great thing when the nearest doctor was at Arisaig from whence it was hard to entice him.

Next day I went down to Smirisary to see what had been done in my absence. Looking down on the house from the crest of the brae, I saw with surprise not the raw metallic sheen of new galvanised iron, but a picturesque expanse of reddish brown, not unlike old tiles. I looked again, and then it dawned upon me that this was rust. The sheets were not galvanised at all but were made of that mild black steel used for Nissen huts, which goes out from the factory without any kind of weather-proofing. The result in our damp Highland climate can easily be imagined. The sheets had been only six weeks in place and were already half rusted through. They had cost me thirteen pounds. According to Jimmy, they were nearly as bad when they came off the train and he had wondered if he should send them back. They would not, he added in his quiet way, last very long. They didn't. Two years later, their remains, scattered about the foreshore by a storm, were too brittle to handle without breaking. But we shall hear of this again.

If the roof was disappointing, the joiner work was beyond praise. Jimmy was a fine craftsman, with a real love of his work, and everything was done in a neat and tradesmanlike manner. There was a smooth, wooden floor in the living-room and an open fireplace with hobs built up with stones and cement. The whole house was lined with planed white boards, with a sheen on them like satin. There were new windows with large panes, and a solid new door.

My next job was to get the place painted and cleaned. I would leave Maisie's house immediately after breakfast, and return at nightfall – a two-mile walk each way. The first day I took a dinner piece, but got such a scolding from Annie that I never dared to do it again. Henceforward, I had both dinner and tea at her house, preceded by a good clean-up with paraffin and hot water. No one ever did me a greater kindness, for of all wretched things the getting of a meal for oneself in the midst of a grimy and exhausting job is the wretchedest. We always spoke in Gaelic; I could already read and write fluently, and was resolved to master the far greater difficulties of conversation. It is to the kindness and long-suffering of my friends in Smirisary and Glenuig, who were willing to hear me murder the tongue of their fathers, that I owe what little skill I may possess in this beautiful and difficult language.

First I painted the roof with black bitumen paint, in the hope of checking the rust. I donned a suit of dungarees, borrowed a ladder, and went aloft with paint-pot and brush, having first scraped off as much rust as I could with a steel brush. If painting is a vile job, scraping is a viler: you are blinded with red dust and the noise would fray the nerves of a Clydeside riveter. I noticed various people watching me discreetly from doorways, for no one had ever seen a woman painting a roof. Angus came to help me shift the heavy ladder from front to back. He was careful to see that the bottom was safely wedged with stones, and his "*Feuch nach tuit thu*" (see that you don't fall) made me sure of the pronunciation of at least one Gaelic phrase. I hate working on ladders; indeed, I had previously been able to avoid it. But now it was inevitable, and the weariness of the work was increased by the strain of overcoming my fear, especially on the top rung of a ladder too short for the job.

But there were compensations. After the storms of summer and early autumn, November came serene and golden. My house faced west, with only the sea before it, so that the afternoon sun lay on it all the year. The nagging wind we had fought so long had fallen and sometimes it was so still that the burnished surface of the sea reflected the slow billowing heave of golden clouds. Astride of the ridge, with black and sticky hands and tarry spatters on my face, I watched the islands change and darken as the sun sank lower and listened to the silky murmur of the swell. Now and again I would see the sleek dark head of a seal, or porpoises rolling by like segments of wheels, and would hear the haunting call of migrating geese far up in the sky. I was quite alone, often tired, but intensely happy, with that serene content which is born of constructive work out of doors; for nothing else, except creative art, gives the same sense of release and fulfilment. Even the roof looked well in its slaty blue-black; I forgot about the rust, though all the time the insidious enemy was working unseen. Then I painted the old wood-work a royal blue, but left the satiny new boards as they were. At last, after a good scrub through, I was ready for the furniture.

This, needless to say, did not amount to much for my own simple plans were made even simpler by the scarcity and dearness of everything. On my return from Glenuig in the spring I had bought a few things in Inverness – a kitchen table, a dresser, two Windsor chairs, and some household utensils. From my mother's house in Ross-shire, now let furnished, I had removed, between tenants, some other things that I thought would not be missed. The goods from Inverness had arrived some weeks before, and were lying at the pier-head under a tarpaulin. When the stuff from Stromeferry had also come, I went to see my neighbour, Alan, who had a large boat, and arranged for the transport of the furniture in two boat-loads. But that was only a beginning. To secure a boat and crew was one thing, but to find a suitable day, with light offshore wind, no swell, and high water at a convenient hour, was another. In winter, the spring tides, which were the best for landing heavy loads at Smirisary, fall awkwardly, high water being between six and eight, too early in the morning and again too late at night.

At last came a fine, calm day, with high water at noon and a light northerly breeze. I met Alan and his son, Angus, at the boat cove, which was called Port an Doicheall, or the harbour of grudging or inhospitality – and well the name suited it. The beach was of coarse shingle, shelving to a rough floor of jagged rock exposed at low water. The only shelter was afforded by a lump of rock called Seann Rudha or Old Point, which at the highest tides became an island. It received the first shock of the waves, and on days of heavy swell the seas would break over it with a shattering roar, as if it were far out in the Atlantic. Other rocks, some tilted and sawlike, some square like ruined castles, rose abruptly from the shingle and grass of the foreshore, their grimness softened by sheets of orange lichen or tussocks of sea pink. Sometimes they were hollowed into caves, often split into fissures called geos,* in which imprisoned waves threw up sudden arms of spray and made loud reports like gun-fire.

The boats, four of them, of various sizes and weights but all solid and with heavy oars, were pulled well above the

---

* Gaelic *geodha* from Norse *gja,* one of the many Scandinavian loan words connected with the sea.

highest tide-mark, each lying in a berth scooped out of the shingle and approached by paths cleared of the largest stones. For the pebbles, if you could call them so, were difficult to walk on and no one with corns should go near Port an Doicheall, especially with a burden on his back. The only convenience was a rude slip built of boulders heaped together, many of the upper ones having been displaced by storms, so that the surface was even worse than the shingle below. The agility with which the men of Smirisary, bred to this work from boyhood, would leap from rock to rock in slippery rubber boots, with heavy loads on their backs, without a slip or a stumble, never ceased to excite my admiration, while I, having come to the place too late, would pick my way cautiously like a cat on hot bricks.

We laid down sticks for the keel to run on, with a little rotten seaweed as lubricant, and soon had the boat at the water's edge. The two men rowed, while I sat idly in the stern watching the progress of a journey that was to become very familiar. Steering with oars alone, we threaded our way through a maze of rocks, some clear of the water, others submerged or awash and the seas breaking over them. We had not gone far before the northerly breeze freshened and steep little waves began to slap against the bows. Alan wanted to turn back, but his son and I persuaded him to go on as the breeze, now against us, would be fair when we returned with our load. After a hardish pull and some water aboard, we loaded the things most urgently needed and returned without incident.

At the shore we were met by one or two neighbours, who helped us to pull up the boat, while Jimmy and Alan's Angus carried up the stuff, so that all I had to do was to unpack and arrange it. Much of the old community spirit survived in Smirisary, for everyone at hand, seeing a local boat come in would hurry to the shore to haul up the boat and carry the cargo.

Certain other things arrived as weather and human

moods permitted. My mother, thinking that I must be tired at night, sent me a spring interior mattress. This, described by one of the men as a "bolster", arrived casually on top of a boat-load of firewood, preserved only by Providence from rolling into the sea. Later on, when I was away for a spell of work at Fernaig, Jean Croll and her friend, Walter, brought a chest of drawers which Jimmy had made out of an old kitchen table and some pieces of plywood. In the same boat was a parcel of clean linen from the laundry. When I returned, I found the chest of drawers in the house, but of the parcel not a sign. I searched high and low, even in the Samalaman boathouse, in case it had been left behind. Finally, I searched the shore, but without much hope, as there had been spring tides and a gale since the boat's coming. About a week later, when I had resigned myself to the loss of three sheets and as many pillow-slips, it happened that Angus Ruairidh* was walking on the shore and saw in the tide-wrack a whitish object, which proved to be a parcel done up with string only, the paper having been stripped off by the waves. I saw him coming up from the shore, with something heavy under his arm and a broad smile on his face. The sheets were intact, though slightly soiled by sand and weed, and inside the pillowslips were several small shrimps. We rinsed all the linen in the burn and then washed it, and it was none the worse. Not often does the sea surrender its spoil so meekly. Not long afterwards I saw in the *Oban Times* an advertisement asking for information about "a chest of drawers, containing clothes, etc., washed off the pier, Isle of Jura, on January 27th". I doubt if the owner of the "clothes, etc.", though equally careless, was as lucky as I.

That first winter I slept, ate, cooked, and lived in the kitchen. I had a good lamp and a comfortable bed, a dresser with a few dishes and books on its shelves, a couple

---

* Angus, the son of Ruairidh (Rory or Roderick Macpherson). There were a great many Anguses on the estate, so it was necessary to distinguish them.

of Windsor chairs, a square of green cork linoleum, and a pair of rugs made of heavy sacks opened out, washed, and adorned with coarse woollen embroidery. The sitting-room was not yet in order and the "closet" at the back, which later became my spare bedroom, I used as a sort of scullery and store-room. The house was bare, almost austere, but I kept it clean and tidy and it soon had an air of home.

As the days shortened, I rose before dawn and have vivid memories of breakfast by lamplight, with the winter day just breaking outside. The bright orange table-cloth and gay crockery were reflected in the uncurtained glass and, through the reflection in curious contrast, I saw an expanse of grey and heaving sea. Though working alone, I was too busy to feel lonely. There was a friendly feeling in the house, as if nothing unpleasant had ever happened there. A Highland house is never entirely abandoned. They leave a Gaelic Bible or, in Catholic places, a holy picture, so that God may be there though man has departed.

My neighbours were very good to me. No one called empty-handed, nor did I ever leave a house without some gift. When I came home from work, I would often find a package of scones or a bottle of milk on the table, and a few potatoes, even peats and kindlings beside the door. People came to see me and asked me to their houses; they gave me good advice and, as a lone woman, I received much help in the heavier work from the men. There remained here, among the older people at least, not only the traditional Highland courtesy, but a measure of that ancient hospitality of Christian men in lonely places, who never turned a stranger from their hearth, lest unawares they should deny their Saviour.

Smirisary was full of ruins, roofless and smothered with brambles; a picturesque sight for late eighteenth-century romance, but a cause of sadness to any lover of the Highlands. The people themselves, though they missed the lighted windows of their youth, took these ruins for granted and found a use for any material they yielded. A diminished township meant more land for those that remained, but there were also fewer to man the boats and less company for the young. Many a Gaelic song is full of the nostalgia of the deserted village:

Tha leac an tein' a nis fas fuar,
Is coinneach ruadh tighinn tkairis. *

There must have been many people here once, though I could learn nothing about the origin of the township. But as it was so crowded and close to the shore, and a bad shore at that, there is little doubt that the people were settled there to make a living from the sea when Glenmoidart was cleared for sheep. There is a tradition that the flat, arable land in the middle of Smirisary was once a swampy *lochan.* Even in the youth of those still living, much fishing was done and large families were the rule; it was no uncommon thing for twelve or fourteen people to live in a two-roomed house.

Now, as in every place on the mainland, there had been a great decline. There were only five households left in Smirisary, all small and mostly consisting of old people. Facing me across the burn were the two Macphersons, brother and sister, both unmarried. A little higher up, under the brae, were two middle-aged bachelor brothers. On a ledge still higher up, lived Alan and his wife, both elderly, and their only son Angus, and Alan's wife's brother. A little apart from the other crofts, to the north, was the Goirtean where, when I first came, Sandy Gillies lived with his married daughter and her two children, for whom the first pram in Smirisary was carried down on her father's back. Now they have gone to Glenuig and there are newcomers at the Goirtean.

---

* The hearthstone is now growing cold, and red moss coming over it.

4

Fire, Water and Bread

THERE was much work to do and only one pair of hands to do it; but as the winter passed I learned my technique. Luckily I had not yet acquired any livestock and thus had more time for getting the croft into some semblance of order. The actual housework did not take me long and my open-fire cookery was of the simplest. But to keep myself supplied with water and fuel involved more labour than you might think.

On ordinary days, when there was no washing or scrubbing, I would use about six gallons, or three large pailfuls – an allowance that would seem princely to the Bedouin but hardly decent to a plumber. Cleaning-water I could get from the burn at the bottom of the little field or, in wet weather, from a hollow behind the house where surface water gathered; but for drinking and cookery I must go to a spring well about 150 yards away. The way to the well, as paths go in Smirisary, was level and easy and the place itself so beautiful that the walk seemed worth while, even if, while gazing at something, you stumbled and spilt the water. The pure, cold spring welled out of the rock into a basin lined with flagstones, which was carefully cleaned out at intervals so that you could dip your pail without gathering a harvest of trailing green weed. As I walked home with a brimming pail in each hand, I would see the green croft land running down to the sea's edge and the busy little burn, fringed with primroses and yellow flags or with meadowsweet and loosestrife in their seasons, and, behind the gable of my house, the peaks of Skye, dim with trailing showers or sharp and clear in the north wind. Twice a day I would visit the well, in the morning and at nightfall; this last was the best time. Then, straightening my back, I watched the quiet end of day beyond the isles, with maybe a young moon setting or a star reflected in the water of the well itself, to be caught in the pail and lost again in the shiver of broken water. In winter, the ground lay still, as if enchanted, showing the footprints of beasts, even the curved marks of last summer's scything, clearer in twilight than ever they were by day. And then I knew for certain what I had never, even in bad times, really doubted – that with all the delays and discomforts, exasperations, and disappointments, it was better to be here than anywhere else at all.

Water-carrying was heavy work, especially when one had a dairy, and a nuisance at the end of a long day, so that I toyed with various schemes for taking water into the house. But gravitation was impossible, rotary pumps an annoyance, and corrugated iron sheets for catching rain-water an eyesore; and so I still walk to the well and, when a few more years have passed, I shall forget that I ever considered anything else. A certain measure of acquiescence in the face of brute facts is necessary if one is to live happily in the Highlands. "Be not too particular; it mars your happiness", once said an old lady, the wife of a former Dean of Canterbury. She must have been a Celt or have lived among them.

Fuel was harder to get than water. I had an occasional bag of coal but transport difficulties made this a precious luxury. You would order say half-a-ton from the store at Lochailort and the hotel lorry would dump it at the pier-head in a little heap, along with other little heaps belonging to other people. Here it would remain until you succeeded in begging, borrowing or stealing ten sacks. In due course, weather permitting, the store-boys would go up to Lochailort, fill the sacks, which were usually rotten and full of holes, and land them either at Glenuig or at Samalaman boathouse. Should there be a storm or an extra high tide, they might be washed off the pier and you would spend the hours at low water gleaning lumps and dross from the sand and seaweed of the ebb.

Those days are gone, and no one regrets them. The estate

now charters a puffer: a year's supply is landed at Samalaman, sold to the crofters and, where possible, delivered
by cart. For those, like ourselves, beyond reach of wheels,
there are heaps of coal lying near Samalaman pier, each
one known to its owner, and from time to time we come in
a boat, with shovels and a collection of old bags, each one
more rotten than the last. We fill them in haste, for fear of
losing the tide, and stow them fore and aft, well out of the
way of the rowers. On top may be logs of firewood or cans of
paraffin or boxes of provisions, fencing stobs, rolls of wire
netting, dogs, and perhaps passengers. And when we reach
Smirisary, and throw the bags ashore, one if not more is
sure to burst, spilling its contents in the boat or over the
gunwale, and groping for coal in seaweed or water, while
daylight ebbs and a stealthy wave washes into your boot, is
the end of many a boat journey.

The natural woods round Samalaman were full of birch,
which could be cut for fuel; and having done much fell-
ing at Achnadarroch and Fernaig, I was not slow to take
my chance here. But if the trees were easily cut, they were
the devil and all to get away. The estate cart could take a
load as far as the Druim, where the County Council road
ended, but it was another half mile farther to Smirisary.
For the first winter I had no pony to carry my burdens and
must rely on my own exertions and the kind offices of my
friends. It was nearly always too stormy to think of going
out in a rowing boat.

The day may come when we cease to complain of the
Smirisary path, either because the authorities have improved it or, more probably, because we are no longer there
to complain. I think it is worth describing in detail, if only
to show how far acquiescence in an avoidable annoyance
could go. From Samalaman to the Druim was a track nomi-
nally kept in repair by the County Council, which could be
used for carts provided that the carter were experienced,
the horse quiet, and the load light and firmly roped. Never-
theless, there were two boggy places, where the peaty soil was

subsiding under the road metal, and a steep brae with a surface like a dry watercourse, where many things have fallen from carts unnoticed because of the deafening rattle of wheels. As for the bogs, I once had to lay down a piece of old wire netting with divots on top before attempting to lead the horse across. At the Druim was a gate separating the Laird's grazing from the crofters', and from this point onwards there was only a footpath, which Dr Fraser Darling described in a letter as "bloody awful". This was an understatement. He saw it only in summer and in daylight: we followed it on winter nights, God help us, with leaky Wellingtons and dud torches.

Below the gate was an abrupt descent of rock and loose stones; then the track crossed the flat of Allt Ruadh, with a surface full of boggy subsidences, one of them dangerous for horses. Next came a rocky staircase, followed by a swamp of overflowing drains from which the weary traveller emerged only to zigzag up the face of a rock till at last, having crossed another wet place with stepping stones, he reached the top of the pass at Faing Mhic Phail. Here, as often as not, he would meet a whistling wind from the sea, bitter with rain or hailstones. After this the path improved for a little, but his hopes were soon dashed by another devil's stairway, followed by a gorge eroded by fifty years of storm. Then more bog and, at last, the steep incline, more like a scree than a track, down which he slithered into Smirisary. In 1894, this misery was a decent footpath made by local labour, with a grant from the Scottish Office. But there was no obligation on anyone to maintain the path, so that everyone considered it someone else's business, blaming the estate, or the County Council, or the crofters, as the case might be. Many a log of birch have I shouldered down that track, and visiting friends made a point of bringing sticks for the fire, as children used once to take with them a peat for the schoolroom hearth.

There was also my peat in the Laran Mor, and this came by another and even more arduous route. In Ross-shire we had always taken home our peats when dry and stored them in a shed. But here it was the custom to build stacks at the bank itself, which were visited once or even twice daily as required. The Laran Mor must be half-a-mile from my house, and a long half-mile; besides the usual slop of mud and scramble of stones, there were ditches to jump and slippery planks to cross. As I had a little wood as well and was very economical with my fire, I went to the stack every second day only, and that was quite enough.

The first time or two I took a creel for the peats, but never again. Creeling is an art that must be learnt young; the elderly beginner will make nothing of it. Though equal with Katie Gillies in size and strength, I found I could manage only half the weight she carried with ease; and in spite of a pad of sacking, the creel jarred my spine and the rope cut my shoulders. Before jumping a ditch, I had to set the creel down and lift it across, and there was no handy rock or bank on which to raise it again. And when, as sometimes happened, I slipped with the thing on my back, I would lie awhile like a capsized beetle, feebly trying to rise and swithering between the desire for someone to come along and the proud hope that they wouldn't. After that I took a sack, which was better, for I could throw the burden across the ditch and swing it up again. But my shoulders were not square enough to keep a heavy sack in the right position for long and at every step the wretched thing would slip lower and lower until I wished all peats and peat mosses at Jericho.

Yet this toilsome plodding and splashing had its compensations. At the top of the pass was a grassy bank on which one could prop the bag and rest without setting it down. Here, with a shock of pleasure that never staled, I came in sight of the wrinkled plains of the sea and the islands sleeping on its breast, and heard again, after the inland silence, its multitudinous and soothing noises. Far below in the crofts, I could see Angus Ruairidh bending over his potatoes and Annie emptying a pail at the door; and I would hear Dane bark as he herded the cows and Alan hammering at his new shed. And then the descent to the level: how kind to my feet was the grass of the croft land, and how welcome the far gable of my house growing larger every minute; and, at last, the doorstep and the bag flung down with a grunt of relief and satisfaction.

Jean Croll had a fine Scottish instinct for storing and laying up treasure, and, feeling that my hand-to-mouth way with the peat was all wrong, she offered to come down with Peggy the milkmaid and we would spend a whole afternoon on the job. We made three journeys, each carrying a bag; and at the end of the day I had nine bags in hand – more than a fortnight's store. The girls were as new to the game as I, and a strange procession we made, stumbling and tumbling down the steep brae, falling into ditches and rising again, with a fine flow of talk and laughter. If we gave the old hands who watched us as much amusement as we found ourselves, we didn't do so badly. The old people say that long ago the peat-carrying, even from distant mosses, was light work because a crowd of youngsters would go together and make a game of it. But now this, like many another crofting job, has become toilsome because the people are few and ageing, and there is no longer comradeship in labour. I was not sorry when the following summer I got a pony, which could carry five times my own load. The peat-carrying left me tired for the rest of the day and the nagging economy of fuel made life in winter rather bleak. On dry days, when I was working outside, I would lunch on bread and cheese and coffee made over a primus, so that I could let out the fire after breakfast and light it again in the evening. This plan saved the big fuel but was heavy on kindlings. Heather was much used by the people but the best sorts were getting scarce near inhabited places and I preferred small driftwood, which, when split and dried, catches in a moment and burns with the merriest of crackles.

Even in war-time, Smirisary was not a good place for driftwood. The islands and the far-flung promontories of Arisaig and Ardnamurchan acted as breakwaters, and little

came to us but bits and pieces. Now and again a north-
westerly gale would drive ashore heavy timber from the
open sea between Rhum and Skye and a few men, who
were out at crack of dawn, got enough to build themselves
a house, had they been so minded, but most of it went
up the chimney. A woman with her housework about her
neck is at a sore disadvantage and, apart from kindlings,
I never got any thing better than a small plank, a smaller
spar, and part of a "dodger" or canvas screen from a ship's
bridge, whereas my neighbours, at one time or another,
have found whole rafts, large battens, pit-props, tarred
rope, petrol tins, and even a barrel of crude vaseline.

The only place near Smirisary where there was much
chance of finding driftwood was Achadh an Aonaich, a surprising little spit of shell sand which recalled, on a small
scale, the white strands of Morar and the Outer Hebrides. Divided by a rocky knoll and strip of green turf were
two sickle-shaped beaches, one looking north-west to Rhu
Arisaig and the Cuillin, the other south-west past Eilean
Shona to Ardnamurchan. Behind, enclosed by precipitous
slopes, was a little *machair* on which, in more crowded and
enterprising days, potatoes were grown. Now it lay abandoned to bracken and rabbits and a few crofters' sheep,
which grazed the clovery sward or picked about among the
seaweed. The foreshore was piled with driftwood already
gathered and appropriated. When I first came, it was safe
to leave anything indefinitely for no local man would touch
what a neighbour had set aside for himself. But later, much
of this store was raided, probably by passing lobster-men.

Often on a fine Sunday afternoon I would go there with
rope and sack to gather driftwood for kindling and, when
I had collected as much as I could carry, would sit leaning against a sandy bank in the westering sun, dreaming in
sleepy content. Only the normally busy person can bring to
perfection the elegant accomplishment of doing absolute-
ly nothing; and for this purpose give me Achadh an Aonaich on a fine Sunday afternoon. In a Catholic community,

the Presbyterian sabbath is not observed and, although Sunday is mostly kept as a day of rest, all are free to amuse themselves after the hours of Mass or to get on with their harvest or any other necessary work.

Across a narrow channel, fanged with skerries, lay two islets, Glas-eilean and Eilean Coille, on which, at certain seasons, Graham ran a few moorit Shetland sheep. They were also the breeding-place of duck and black-backed gulls, and boats from Smirisary would visit them in May to gather eggs. Both islands were treeless and only a few feet above sea level, being covered with heather and incredibly lush green grass, fertilised by the salt spray and the droppings of birds. Above the tide-mark was a fringe of corn, chickweed, and other mainland plants whose seeds were carried out to sea by floods. The nests, mere hollows scooped in the grass, were soon found and the large, prettily speckled eggs collected in pails. Before leaving we would test them for freshness in a pool near the shore and all that failed to float were discarded. A fresh gull's egg is very good, much like a hen's only larger, and with no taste of fish. They should be boiled for a quarter of an hour.

As a crofter, I was sorry that Achadh an Aonaich was over a mile from the township and approached by a track too narrow and precipitous even for a hill pony, for its shell sand, and even more the coral sand that is found on an *oitir* or bank a little farther south, could be used in place of lime; in the old days, boats from Skye and other places came regularly in search of it. A boat is the only way; and by this time the reader will know that it is one thing to speak of boats and quite another to launch them. The path – a mere broken sequence of sheep tracks – was wild and wet and to a stranger very difficult to follow. On every side were rocks and chasms and gorges, with the sea moaning far below. A frightening place on a gloomy winter's evening and in a westerly gale a cruel lee shore. But nothing comes close inshore but small local craft, which only go to sea in good weather.

Between Achadh an Aonaich and Smirisary, well hidden from view in a gully, was a cave about forty feet long and ten feet wide and perfectly dry. At the entrance you could see the ruins of an illicit whisky still, and there is no doubt that barley was brought from the Outer Isles and landed on the sandy beach, from which it could easily be carried to the cave. At the time of the Clearances, a family evicted from Glenmoidart lived for some time in this dry and spacious shelter. Later, it was used as a store for bracken by three crofters who shared the hill-ground above it. They carried it home to the byres as required, and in my early days, when I was still unused to the path, I would follow the trail made by fragments of bracken that fell from their burdens.

In the winter of 1942, paraffin was very scarce. We were rationed to half-a-gallon a week per household, with one candle and one box of matches. At the Big House, large rooms were lighted by single candles, and people went down the big corridors with torches or nightlights or cycle lamps. Thus, though I had a primus stove, I rarely used it, except for the lunch coffee, and would cook over the fire I sat by, which was well enough for boiling kettles or making toast, but not so good for frying or baking on the girdle, especially if you wanted to keep two pots going at once. The Crolls's excellent meals were mostly prepared on the dining-room fire, where Mrs Croll would make a dinner for eight, skilfully balancing a collection of pots, pans, and kettles, kneeling endlessly on the hearthrug to stir their contents. As for me, I found my own one-woman household quite enough, for even in solitude I demand square meals. No snack of tea and scones will generate in me the energy required for outdoor work.

Two years later I was able to get a two-burner "Florence" oil cooker and a permit for a forty-gallon drum of paraffin. This sounds well on paper but in practice you do not get more than your ration; indeed, as things turned out, I was likely to get a good deal less. The drum was landed at Samalaman pier and, being too heavy to handle in the small boat, we arranged to leave it where it was and draw off the paraffin as required. Walter, a friend of Graham's, came to help me fill a number of petrol cans which could be taken to Smirisary on the pack-saddle. But the oil spouted forth with such violence that it drenched our corduroy trousers, so that we became obnoxious to our friends for several days. Then came a high equinoctial tide, which floated the drum off the jetty, and but for Walter's devotion it would have followed the Jura chest of drawers to its unknown end. At this point it seemed safer to empty the paraffin into a superannuated container I had brought from my old home. But the container was rusty, and before long developed a slow leak so that we had to decant the remainder into Mrs Croll's drum, which luckily was not very full. After that I was thankful to return to weekly driblets in tins and cans, leaving to others the worry of large-scale operations.

If I have been too prolix about fuel, it is only because it means so much to us. Better to be warm and hungry than full and cold. In the moist West Highland climate, where one's feet are always wet and one's clothes perennially damp, a fire is a necessity, even in summer, so small blame to the crofter if he is haunted by the fear of an empty hearth. "Come away in to the fire" is the standard invitation; and the neighbours' frequent enquiries about my fuel supply and their gifts of peat and kindlings all point the same way. An artist I know was seething with indignation because the crofters saw nothing in trees but firing and cut down everything within easy reach of their houses, thus stripping the land of shelter as well as of beauty. So it is; and many a sound plank won from the sea has roared up Sandy's chimney, to be regretted later when he wanted wood for making or mending. But there is no help for it.

In peace-time it was not really difficult to get provisions, even in remote places like Smirisary, provided that one learned the technique of shopping by post and remembered to place the orders in time. We had sacks of flour and oatmeal and sugar, and large tea-boxes of groceries, and barrels of salt herring, and the rest we supplied ourselves. But the war changed all that. Rationing is bad enough in town, where the housewife visits the shops in person. But in the remote Highlands it is the devil and all. Ration books are deposited with distant retailers over whom the customer has no check; he must take what comes to him without power of choice or change. The weekly system gives no chance of building up a store against bad weather and broken communications, the very essence of island and Highland economy. We struggle in a mesh of petty regulations and restrictions, like dying flies in a spider's web. The last indignity has been the pointing of oatmeal, the crofter's staple food. "I can't think", said Angus, "what is happening to the Kingdom." Well might he wonder. Our Minister of Food means well, poor soul; but if he ever comes here, he should carry a phial or two of cyanide in his hat. I could write a lot more about this, but it is unnecessary. The reader, who also has suffered, will understand.

When I first came to Smirisary, there was still a shop at Glenuig, but rationing had reduced it to a shadow. It was open only on Fridays, and Mrs MacDonald was continually threatening to close it altogether, which in the end she did. Every Thursday the week's supply of Glasgow bread and rationed goods would arrive at Lochailort station, whence it was carried by lorry to the pier and loaded on the storeboat. In theory the rations were not distributed until the next day; but so great was our eagerness to replenish well-scraped sugar-bowls and empty tea-caddies, that most people besieged the shop on Thursday evening, and its small space was clamorous with dogs playing and fighting under the counter and among the legs of the customers. There was a great buzz of conversation and counting, the talk being in Gaelic and the reckoning in English. The quiet emptiness of Glenuig would be broken by strings of people coming down the glen or along the shore, with white flour-bags on their backs in which the rations were carefully stowed. All the horses in the place were often seen at once: the estate cart, with the white garron in the shafts and the young grey following loose, would rumble over the plank bridge, while the Allt Ruadh pony, hitched to the shop door, would exchange snaps and squeals with Blossom, my mare.

When the shop closed, both Maisie Bright and I were asked to reopen it. I cannot imagine any ploy I would like less, or any job more thankless than keeping a village store in war-time. The clerical work of rationing falls heavily on the small shop-keeper, who is not only unaccustomed to such labour, but has usually many other duties and cares. He – or more often she – is also blamed for all disappointments and delays, though these may be caused not by the weather, nor even by Hitler, but by the working of some uncomprehended economic law, or merely by the present state of the universe. If ever there is riot or revolution in the glen, with battle, murder and sudden death, it will not be for the sake of captains and kings, nor for any racial or political issue, but because the sugar has gone amissing, and no one can explain why.

5

Byre and Barn

THAT first winter I lived alone, without even a cat for company. Having come so late in the season, I could not cut hay or raise any crop for wintering, nor had I as much as a shed to house a beast. There had once been a byre and a barn, but when a croft goes derelict the drystone outhouses are the first to fall into ruin. A stone falls here and there and no one replaces it; the sag in the roof becomes a gaping hole; little by little the rotten thatch collapses, and neighbours strip the timbers for fuel or repairs. A few years of storm and neglect will reduce a useful outbuilding to a roofless rain, enclosing a mass of weeds and brambles. Smirisary was full of these dismal wrecks, and when looking for a place to house a cow and pony, I was not surprised to find three possibilities within a few yards of the house. Of these, one was rejected as too damp and dilapidated, though later on it provided a quantity of blocks and flagstones for other constructions. Another, though well-preserved and very dry, was on the far side of an abrupt little gully, which would be awkward to cross with milk pails at night. The third was at right-angles to the house and so near it that the long walls of each building formed an L which sheltered the garden plot from east and north. The walls were in fairly good order, though they needed raising in some places and strengthening in others, and as the overall measurement was less than that of the dwelling house, I was able to use the soundest of the old galvanised sheets for the roof. I had of course to provide new timbers, the old ones having long since disappeared.

The first and toughest job was to clear the interior. The old rush thatch had fallen in and, mingling with peat dust and decayed vegetation, had produced a layer of black soil a foot deep, in which there grew a thicket of brambles and nettles as high as your head. Maisie, who loved such ploys, came down one afternoon to help me. Arrayed in her oldest waterproof, hedging gloves and Wellingtons, she cut the brambles root and branch, while I cleared the rubbish with a graip. We sang as we worked, and thoroughly enjoyed ourselves. The next stage – shovelling away the soil – was not so pleasant, and no one volunteered to help. A dozen years of Highland rain had packed it close and the roots of bramble and nettle formed a network which in many places ran beneath the flagstones of the floor and through the chinks of the wall. Indeed, long after the byre was roofed and sheltered a cow, pale spindly shoots kept coming up, though heaven alone knows what kept them alive. Mixed with the earth were small stones fallen from the wall, and little lumps of coal and fragments of peat and rotten sticks and bits of rusty wire. Between backache and nettle-stings and the confined space, I have never done a harder or less agreeable job of work. The soil was all taken out in a barrow and used to make a herbaceous border.

Then Alan, who was an excellent drystone mason, came to raise and straighten the walls. We spent a couple of days at this work, I gathering the stones and he laying them. Many of those we needed were lying beside the wall from which they had fallen; but a few extra ones we carried or wheeled from the other ruins and I was kept busy collecting small flat slabs for packing. Then Alan cemented in one of the old windows from the house and, in exchange for the other one, produced a door of his own, which served with but little alteration.

Then I procured timber from the sawmill at Kinlochmoidart, and Jimmy put on the roof. He worked at top speed, with only myself as assistant, and was quite ruthless in his demands: no "See you don't fall" or any softness of that sort. I was persuaded to stand on a ladder, laid horizontally across the walls, and support the ridge beam while he nailed the rafters. There was no spare wood for making stalls but Angus MacNeil had found a long, thick plank on the shore; this I begged from him, and we used it to make a partition between the cow's stall and the pony's. Thus I had a good byre and stable combined, complete with drain and flagstone floor. For some months it remained empty and made a useful shelter for wood-cutting, carpentry, and other odd jobs. At the time of writing, the byre houses two cows, a heifer, and a calf: the pony has a stable to itself.

The barn problem was not so easy to solve. There was no hope of repairing either of the adjacent ruins – wood was too scarce and dear. Then I remembered a derelict cottage on the shore, which had stood empty for many years and was stripped of all woodwork but the roof timbers and the door. The little place had never been a croft house, but was built about fifty years ago, on the crofters' grazing and by their own labour, for an old woman who lived there alone. When she left, it was used at first to house sheep in the winter and later as a communal store for boat gear. The walls were of solid unmortared stone; there was a single fireplace with a central chimney and a galvanised iron roof with blunt ends. The sheets were thick with rust and ragged at the edges, and the ridging, rusted away from the nails, flapped drearily in the wind. But no rain seemed to penetrate, for everything inside was as dry as a bone. The flagstones of the floor, which according to Angus were specially fine ones, were now covered with a hard layer of old sheep-dung. One of the two rooms was full of oars, spars, and sails, but the other was empty and would hold all the hay I was likely to scrape together. The door, being too rotten to hang, lay sideways across the entrance, jammed in position with stones. This was an infernal nuisance, as the stones were heavy to shift, and the door usually fell flat on your feet as you stooped to lift them. So, after enduring this for some time with much grousing and no attempt to find a remedy, as the way is in the West, I finally sawed off the rotten part and made a half-door of it, complete with hinges contrived out of bits of old harness, and a wooden sneck to close it.

The little house stood in a green recess with a low but precipitous cliff behind it, and was called Toll Uaine, or the Green Hole. It was not more than two minutes' walk from my byre, along an easy grassy path, as paths go in Smirisary. Though facing the open sea and not more than a few feet above it, the place was always sheltered, even in a westerly gale, for the cliff behind made a pocket of calm, the wind flowing upwards over the top. From the gaping windows, long since stripped of wood and glass, you could look right into the breakers and see the sunset through the spray.

Often on late summer evenings I would lie for a while on the sweet-smelling pack of newly-stored hay, and gaze upon the slow swell rolling shoreward, and on the islands riding the sea, and, far beyond, upon a line of shining cumulus clouds, whose base, below the horizon, rested on the peaks of Heaval in Barra and of Ben More in South Uist. And I would think of Ceit Mhor,* and try to reconstruct her life in the house that is now my barn. Her henhouse, with its lintel made of a single slab of stone, was still intact, though bracken and brambles grew thick within it. The well she used was now choked with mud and water-weed, but its overflow seeped down to the sea, fanning out into a shallow green marsh where cattle loved to graze in the heat of summer. When, during the spring drought of 1946, I cleared this well to make a drinking place for the cows, Angus told me that it was called Tobar Mhairearead, or Margaret's well; so there is no need for me to change the name. I asked people to tell me about Ceit Mhor, and they said that she was a good neighbour and her house much frequented for *ceilidh*; she was handy with a creel, and always ready to pull with the men when a boat's keel was heard grating on the shingle. Though only a short distance from the neighbours, no house could be seen from her doorstep but the white ones far away on Eigg, bright in the morning sun.

One could not be long in this land without falling into

* Big Kate.

a mood of brooding reminiscence. The whole place was full of memories and our awareness of them, even when the details were unknown. Every rock and burn had its Gaelic name, often commemorating some person or event; Faing Mhic Phail (Mac Phail's Fold) where a man called MacPhail died suddenly while herding; Glac nan Lion (The Hollow of the Nets) where fishermen used to spread their nets for repair. Sandy Gillies told me that he would often flee from the uproar of house-cleaning or wailing babies to the shore or the hill, and think about the old days, when people were poorer than they are now but much gayer and more contented. I would often see him at the day's ending, his head and shoulders black against the bright sky, on top of the steep knollie called Crnoc Man a' Churaich, between his house and mine. The cows were grazing below, and they made a good excuse for sitting; but he had not gone there to herd but to meditate. The turf at the summit was worn by the feet of many generations, coming to watch cattle, or observe the tide, or study the weather, or scan the sea for signs of returning boats or approaching shoals of fish, or merely to see what their neighbours were doing. Now Sandy has gone and no one seems to go there but myself.

At the time of writing, I have just finished putting my fourth season's crop of hay into the little house on the shore. Since Ceit Mhor went out, it has made a good shelter for sheep, for hay and the tackle of boats. But I hope that one day I may be able to put it in order as a dwelling-house. A fine place to grow old in, with hoary rocks and endless sequence of tides to teach you patience. A place where it would not be too hard to learn that last lesson in detachment – to let the young go their way in peace, and render up, without fuss or repining, the power and place we no longer can nor ought to retain.

In front of my barn and beyond it, lay a good trace of maritime grazing, which Sandy and I once shared but which later became mine alone. When cattle were more numerous, it was all green but, in after years, bracken and heather began to creep in, the choked well was souring the ground about it, and there was too much ragwort and too many rabbits. Above the boat harbour was another ruin, full of brambles, which once, in the palmy days of Smirisary, housed the crofters' bull. There were also ancient folds of various sizes, where perpendicular rock faces were joined by crumbling walls of loose stones, so as to form green enclosures for stock at night. In the old times, crofters' cattle were never housed in byres in summer as they are to-day. From dawn to dusk they grazed on the hill, attended by a herdsman who took his turn with the rest. Then, at the darkening, they were brought home, milked, and kept in a fold till morning. When I first saw the low walls of the folds – some were not more than eighteen inches high – I wondered how so slight a barrier would serve for beasts accustomed to roam the hill. But Angus said that they were so full of grass, they had no wish to move. And I have found by experience that a very low drystone wall will keep back cattle, because they are afraid of dislodging the stones.

At the north end of this grazing was a narrow gap in the rocks leading to the Faing Mor or Great Fold – a more modern enclosure with high walls where, not so long ago, the crofters' sheep were gathered. Beside it was another and larger enclosure, with the sea on three sides and a rock face on the fourth. Like all places where sheep have ever been penned, it was full of sweet grass and wild white clover and, being approached by a narrow pass which could be closed with a bar, Sandy would often fold his cattle there on hot summer days, when flies made them restless or when he and his household were away for a few hours. Later, on my becoming the sole occupier, I used the Faing Mor as a night field for the cows in summer. In the lingering June twilight, I would saunter behind them, prodding them through the gap and into the passage, where there was only just room for them to walk in single file; their white flanks, bulging with grass, would scrape the rocky walls. Then, as they emerged into the wide enclosure, Brigid would turn right and rub her neck against a stone, while Daisy stood motionless, staring at the sea. I would lean on the wooden bar and watch the curve of their horns, graceful as a young moon, darken as the light was drained from the west, and listen to the vast sighing that went up from the heaving waste of waters. Sometimes I would stay until the cows wandered off to find the resting place of their choice, for in that amphitheatre of rock there was shelter from every wind. And very occasionally – for I am no Spartan in this matter – I would bathe in the shelving pebbly cove on the north side, where stealthy swells crept in and out among the boulders they had polished smooth.

6

The Garden
and the Blaran Boidheach

I. The Garden

ON the far side of the byre, and handy to the midden, was a small walled garden, which had been there as long as anyone could remember. There was no gate, but a neat gap closed by the inevitable bedstead rail. When I first saw this garden, it had been out of cultivation for several years, and had reached that stage – so much more forbidding than mere wildness – when the whole surface was a tangle of dockens, couch grass, buttercup, and ragwort, adorned with trailing festoons of bramble and here and there a bristling Scotch thistle. There was also a moribund gooseberry bush, a willow long past its prime, a couple of those crabbed elder trees that grow like weeds round old buildings, a wind-vexed thorn, and a multitude of nettles.

Though neither walls nor bushes were of any height, the garden, like the barn, was curiously sheltered. You could work there in a westerly gale, with great waves crashing on the rocks below, and hardly feel a breath. It was in full view of the main Smirisary path and as I dug I could exchange news with passing neighbours. But it needed, and would need for many years more, an appalling amount of labour. In this damp, mild climate the seeding rate of weeds and their baleful vitality must be seen to be believed. A hoe, unless used almost every day, is useless; you must grub the wretched things out with a fork and remove them from the garden, for if left to wither on the ground they take root again, and if buried in the orthodox fashion they will soon force their way to the surface. The old stone walls were so far off the straight that I could not lay the rabbit-netting flush against them; and between wall and netting was a space too narrow to cut or clean, in which dockens, nettles, and brambles flourished exceedingly. There was also a climbing plant with an odd sticky texture, of which I have been unable to learn the name.

The first summer I grew a variety of vegetables and even two rows of strawberries. These last bore but little fruit, which was just as well for the rotten herring-net with which they were covered was walked upon by a cow and wherever she set her foot a hole appeared. Later, a section of the wall was knocked down by a neighbour's pony. No damage was done, as it was winter, but it took Angus and Sandy a whole day to repair the breach.

The following spring, having turned some fresh ground in front of the house, I decided to devote the old garden to fruit, and made a fruit cage which contained seven rows of strawberries, five of raspberries, and eight black currant bushes. Maisie and I cut birch poles in the woods and dug them in. In that shallow soil, it was difficult to get them set firmly and we strengthened them with wire guys fixed to posts outside the walls. The sides of the cage were made of wire netting, six feet high, and the top of herring net. I now supposed myself safe from aggression, until Dileas, my collie, leapt over the wall and right through the net, leaving a ragged rent which Angus, who had been a fisherman, mended very neatly for me. The strawberries were luscious and I had a bowl of them with sugar and cream daily. But cleaning the rows was a nightmare. Never have I seen more succulent chickweed, more tenacious buttercups, or groundsel so prolific. The rushes I laid down in default of straw harboured slugs innumerable. Later, when the fruit was over, runners seemed to sprout as fast as one broke them off.

As I toiled among the rows, I began to see why the Highlander rarely troubles to grow vegetables. A few households had small plots, which were hastily dug in May, when the other spring work was finished, and planted with cabbage and perhaps a row or two of carrot and turnip. But the majority raised nothing but potatoes – even those who had worked in the gardens of the gentry and had not the excuse of ignorance. Vegetables are very good on the table, but the work they make, both indoors and out, is unbelievable until you try. I often wonder why I grow them myself – whether it is from pure greed, or pride, or because I happen to like working with a spade. Years ago, I vowed that I would have a house standing on the open hill, without cultivation or enclosure, while now I must needs have a garden, not established even but made from scratch and expanding every year. The thing grows, like a disease; it becomes impossible to stop, or even to retrench, and I find myself envying my neighbours who have never begun.

When I first saw my house, there was a stretch of rough turf in front of it, with nettles and burdocks growing up to the threshold. In English fashion I wanted my garden close at hand, so that I could see it as I washed the dishes, instead of banished to some obscure corner, as it is so often in Scotland. So I decided to fence the nearer part of the grass and plant it with vegetables and flowers.

The first winter I did no more than make a pathway in front of the house, a narrow border under the windows, and a wider one under the byre wall. I also turned a small plot for early potatoes. Both borders were enriched with soil taken from inside the byre. The wide one was a success from the first. It faced south and was sheltered not only by the byre wall, but also by a short dyke at the seaward end made from stones lifted from the potato patch. It now contains, among other things, immensely tall hollyhocks and delphiniums, which have to be elaborately staked against the wind. But the narrow one was a failure; and the following year I replaced it with a pavement made from flagstones gathered from various ruins and bedded in gravel from the brae at the back. The gravel, though very near at hand, was hard to work as the ground was too steep for a barrow and I had to carry it in pails – a slow business and sore on the back.

The second autumn I dug another border, running the full length of the house and separated from the pavement by a strip of grass which was kept short with a scythe. Here I planted some hardy perennials, but not many survived the trampling they got a few weeks later when, with disastrous suddenness, the house had to be re-roofed. The reader may remember that I had a handsome gatepost, but no gate. Timber being scarce, I contrived a rustic gate of interwoven hazel rods, which lasted four years, though the inward list of the gatepost prevented me from hanging it straight. Indeed, the post, which leans a little farther every year, will probably collapse before the plaited hazel is replaced by something smarter and more rectangular.

The following spring I trenched the rest of the enclosure and planted potatoes. It was heavy work. I broke up the bottom of each trench with a pick and removed pailfuls of stones of every size and shape. Flat and square ones were reserved for building, while the small and odd-shaped were piled into a ramp at the seaward end to break the wind. In one corner I laid bare the foundations of some ancient building – large rectangular blocks, lime and rubble, broken crockery, and the shells of winkles innumerable which the inmates had used for food or bait. In the upper and stonier part of the ground the potatoes did well but below, where the soil appeared deeper and richer, they failed completely. Later, when digging a drain there, I found a spring bubbling up from the rock below, and when the water had been diverted into a channel, and the ground well limed, this part of the garden became as good as the rest. In that season, both flower borders delighted the eye in spring and summer, though dahlias and other autumn blooms were badly punished by the buffeting and spindrift of a September gale. I have since planted a shelter hedge of Cotoneaster Simonsii.

The third winter, I dug a piece of waste ground between

the old garden and the byre and cleared a little jungle of nettles and brambles on the far side of it. Then, with the help of Maisie and Angus, I built two stone dykes to enclose the new intake and connect it with the old walled garden on the north and the new fenced garden on the south. The building of these dykes gave me great pleasure. The stones, trundled in the barrow from the large ruin which served us as a quarry, were mostly flat or square and ready to use. We took out a shallow trench about three feet wide and laid the larger and squarer stones in two parallel rows, filling the space between with rubble. The courses should come in slightly as they rise, so that the top of the dyke is a little narrower than the base. If the foundation stones lie true and are well wedged, and any loose or fallen ones are replaced as soon as spotted, a drystone dyke may last a lifetime, though a subsidence of the ground caused by frost or excessive rainfall may make it list or even collapse. In these days of shoddy substitutes and work half done, it is a pleasure to use material, like stone or thatching straw, which comes to us whole, as God made it, and gives no excuse for scamping.

This bald chronicle hardly does justice to what had always, even in its toughest and most disappointing moments, brought me the authentic joy of constructive work. It was all good, from the first stirring of a new idea to the lingering contemplation of the finished thing, so far from what I planned but the best I could do. It was all good, but for two regrets: that there was no one to share the planning and the pleasure, and that there were so many things that my sex, age, and single-handedness put out of reach. The boat that could not go to sea without a man to help; the stone so well suited to my purpose that must be left behind because I could not lift it alone; the framework of a shed that was off the square because there was no one to steady it while I drove in the nails. Yet, little by little, one thing was finished and another begun, and I learned to be content with small gains and slow advances, and not to talk about anything until it was an accomplished fact. I wanted the croft to be not merely a home for one woman, but a plot of Highland earth left better than I found it, by way of thanks for all the kindness I received from people and for all the pleasure I got from the sea and the hills themselves.

I am afraid that I am but a poor and ignorant gardener. Planning a garden, even the peaceful and humdrum job of digging it, is one thing; but fiddling with small seeds, and the everlasting war against weeds, slugs, and caterpillars is quite another. Yet my earliest recollection, as a child of two, was of a field of potatoes in bloom; and being reared among the College gardens of Oxford, I always loved flowers and knew their names. Young people do not as a rule care for gardening; and when I became mature enough to develop this taste, I found myself involved in the endless work of a small farm. And farmers, who spend their lives outside and in contact with earth, do not find their recreation in more earth, but in a pleasant fug indoors. It takes a sedentary worker to reach a really fine pitch of gardening enthusiasm. My own chief delight has been in the flowers of the wild: bluebells among curled croziers of young bracken; foxgloves after a shower, new-washed in sudden sunshine; glimmering sheets of bog-cotton in the June midnight. There is nothing in a garden to touch the elusive beauty of these.

But garden flowers that seem common, even blatant, in a suburb acquire, like daily things transfigured by moonlight, a new and exciting quality when made to grow among wild rocks and seas, waving their frail, gallant banners in the storm. In the same way there was pleasure – and it was something more than perverse defiance – in growing flowers as well as vegetables in war-time, in spending money and labour on something that would neither feed our friends nor kill our enemies, but merely gladden the eye of either. So I was not inclined to apologise for a pot of flowers beside the porridge.

The first winter I spent much time with wheelbarrow and pails, just picking things up and trundling them away –

stones, bits of scrap iron, old tins, straw, sawdust, broken glass, rags, and I know not what, as well as the roots of the dockens, thistles, and nettles which I had clawed up round the house and byre. It does not sound much, but it took time and labour, nor was it easy to get the stuff out of sight. Much of the ground was too soft or too rocky even for my light galvanised barrow, and most of the day seemed spent in the filling, carrying and emptying of pails.

It was not long before I found a young assistant. Alec, the six-year-old grandson of Sandy Gillies, was not yet at school and spent most of his time in going from one croft to another in search of entertainment. The wheelbarrow enchanted him and he would spend hours pushing it about, loaded with a few small stones or handfuls of rubbish. Each day came a knock at the door and the eternal question: "*Am bheil sibh dol a dh' obair leis a' bharra-roth an diugh?*" (Are you going to work with the wheelbarrow to-day?) He was supposed to be helping me, but it did not always work out like that, as I often had to stop to lift the wheel over some rough place which the youthful navvy could not tackle alone. He always put in more than he could push and, when I suggested that the load was too heavy, he replied that he liked things heavy. Then suddenly he would drop the handles, and exclaiming, "'*S' fhearr dhomh falbh!*" (I had better go), would vanish over the pass.

Often when working in the garden or about the house, I would see some of the men go down to the Port and presently hear the grinding of keel on shingle – a noise that to me is like the sound of battle to a war-horse. And then perhaps I would turn away my eyes, so as not to see the boat launched and away, with oars smiting the sea in order. It always gives me a pang to watch a boat put off without me – the same pang I felt in childhood when, with nose pressed against the nursery pane, I heard the fading clip-clop of the hansom that bore my mother away to a party; or, later, when I saw a sweetheart go off on some ploy from which I was excluded. I used to think that age would dull those pangs, but it never has – even when I know that the boat is only going to Samalaman for coal or a few hundred yards along the shore to collect bags of winkles.

Sometimes in the late autumn, when the herring came into Loch nan Uamh, Sandy Gillies and Angus Ruairidh and Angus Alan would go away with the flood tide in Alan's black boat with the brown sail and set their net at dusk, returning in the small hours with their silvery harvest. It was more than once suggested that I should go with them, but feeling pretty sure that they would rather not be bothered with a woman at sea, I made some excuse and contented myself with giving them sardines to take with them for supper, and eating some of the herring they brought back.

The grinding of the keel! The thought that I might have married a man who could (and would) sail a boat is one of the few things that makes me regret the single state. But he would no doubt have refused to take me with him or, even if he took me, would not have allowed me to touch anything, like the sailor in the Somerset folk-song, who, when his young woman wished to accompany him, advised her to stay safely ashore, for:

> Your pretty little hands can't handle our tackle,
> And your pretty little feet on our topmast can't go.

How true! But at the same time how exasperating!

II. The Blaran Boidheach

The enclosure next the house, whose Gaelic name means "the pretty little field", might have been one and a quarter acres in extent, but its irregular shape made it hard to measure. Fenced on three sides by a low, casually piled, drystone dyke and on the fourth by a more or less sheer drop to the foreshore, it was one of the queerest places imaginable. It contained the two large ruins already mentioned – one of a barn, with all four walls intact, the other of a dwelling house, which was occupied within living memory. The barn I intended some time to restore; but the house, built on a damp site and far more ruinous, was of no use but to provide stones for other constructions, and many of these were too heavy to remove without splitting. How some of them were raised without tackle, as no doubt they were, is a mystery. As everyone says, the old people must have been immensely strong and, of course, numerous. We, their dwindling and feeble descendants, find it hard enough to dislodge the stones they raised. Or perhaps it is the will that is weak.

There were also the remains of four smaller and rougher buildings made of loose stones thrown together anyhow. They may have been no more than folds for sheep or cattle but no one remembered them in use. The ground was further broken up by a number of humps and knollies, some natural, others made of stones gathered from the land when it was first cleared, and gradually overgrown with turf. In the corner nearest the house was a steep gully, whose northern face was made damp and rushy by a seeping of water from some hidden spring. Apart from these irregularities, the Blaran was fairly level, and carried good grass which has been greatly improved by four years' mowing and grazing and heavy dressings of dung and seaweed.

This little park was so useful and handy to the house that I spent much time and labour in improving it. The first year I dug a main drain running diagonally from a wet patch in the north-east corner to the bottom of the gully, with an outlet to the shore. This was fed by smaller lateral drains to carry off the water from the north slope. These drains were open, for tiles are expensive and need a skilled drainer to lay them. Thus the rushy sides and floor of the gully became reasonably dry and the following year I limed and turned the ground, and sowed a good grass mixture, which took well, though how long it will stand remains to be seen.

I was long in solving the problem of the rains, which were not only an eyesore, but occupied much precious space and hindered cultivation. The large buildings, being on the edge of the field and out of the way, I left as they were. But the four small ones were out in the middle, and a constant annoyance when mowing or manuring. Their walls were only a foot or two high, but immensely wide, and with the ring of half-buried fallen stones and coarse unpalatable weeds that surrounded them, wasted many square yards of useful ground. Inside was a circle of good grass, but there was hardly room to swing a scythe, and Angus insisted on cutting it himself for fear I should break the point. The old people would have used a sickle – traditionally a woman's implement – which will go where a scythe will not; but it needs expert handling, and the novice may easily cut himself badly. It is tedious work too and I have always refused to learn.

At last I could bear the sight of those ruins no longer and started with a pick to demolish the largest and most irritating of the four. But I had not gone far before it became plain that one woman would take a very long time to shift so many tons of stone. So I persuaded the two brothers, Angus and Sandy MacNeil, to do the job for me. They were very quick workers, and strong. I helped them with the small stones and it took the three of us a week. The best blocks were used to raise the boundary dyke and the rest we threw into a corner. This year, at hay-time, a smooth expanse of grass delighted the eye and the scythe swished through it without hindrance or danger. As I write, the garden has begun to encroach on the Blaran – a process to which there seems to be no end. When I first came to Smirisary, there was, at the seaward end of the gully, one of those "awful corners" that are found somewhere on every farm or croft. Here my predecessors had dumped the ashes of their peat fire, and in the course of time, when the place was left to itself, the ashy surface weathered and turned to soil, in which there grew an amazing crop of nettles, burdock, and couch grass. These weeds were waist-high and the burdock, with its twelve inches of root, was so prolific that in autumn the heads and switches of the cows were plastered with burrs. The time came when I could endure the sight of that jungle no longer. In the third winter I cleared it all, root and branch, dug over the ground, limed it, and in the following spring planted potatoes. They were excellent, and if all goes according to plan they will be followed by cabbages and sprouts.

There were also, near the sea, three other pieces of land, for my croft, like most of the others, was very scattered. At this point for the sake of those who do not know the Highland crofting system, I had better explain. The land belongs to the proprietor, who receives the rent and still enjoys a certain amount of prestige, though his claws have been cut very short by Act of Parliament. It is occupied by the crofter, who, provided that he pays his rent and does not flagrantly misuse his holding, cannot be evicted and may even will the croft to a near relative. Disputes between landlord and tenant or between two tenants are settled by the Scottish Land Court, a body on the whole more favourable to the crofters. In a crofting township, the arable land is held severally and the hill grazing in common, and the "souming" or number of sheep, cattle, and horses allowed to each man is limited, though at the present day the dwindling population has made these restrictions less important. In larger and more prosperous communities, there is an increasing demand for arable ground all in one piece and within a ring fence, for without continuous enclosures there can be no progress. But in the remoter townships, the old system of scattered pieces – devised to give each man a fair share of the land, good, bad and indifferent – still remains. In Smirisary there were some plots, no more than a few square yards in area, carefully marked off with stones or rods stuck in the ground. My own holding contained no less than six different pieces. Of these, only one adjoined the house, while two, and those the largest, were out of sight of the homestead and a good 500 yards away up a steep hill.

51

The three pieces by the sea were all in good cultivation, for being mixed up with Sandy's croft at the Goirtean, it had been worth his while to manure and mow them for himself until some fresh tenant appeared. All three yielded a good crop of hay the first summer and an even better one the second. The largest and best of them lay just below Sandy's well and had easily-spotted boundaries, so that there was no need to mark it with rods or stones. Its only disadvantage was that a footpath crossed it. Now footpaths across crofters' arable are taken very seriously, for land is precious, and the numerous tracks – from house to house, from house to well, from house to shore – waste quite a bit of it. You must be careful always to walk in the same place, even in winter, and when spreading manure to leave the path undunged. I always admired the neatness with which my neighbours marked the edges of the blank green ribbon that wound its way among the brownish speckled surface of the manured meadowland.

I always enjoyed working at the Goirtean, not only for the beauty of the place itself, but for the pleasant company I found there. Sandy and his married daughter Katie were always about, doing the same work at the same time, and we would help one another, and talk as we worked, and at the end of it there would often be a cup of tea at the narrow, well-scrubbed table in the window. My cow – I had only one at first – used to run with theirs, and they told me not to worry about her for they would herd her with their own. Each household supplied the needs of the other; and when in the spring of 1946 Sandy left the Goirtean, I knew that I had lost one of the best of neighbours. As Angus said: "We were boys at school together, and from that day to this we never had a cross word. I never had to ask him for anything – he would come to help without being bidden."

Though the Goirtean was only three minutes' walk from my house, the prospect was quite different, for the ground sloped to the north, and I could see the surf breaking on the skerries of Rhu Arisaig and, far beyond, the visionary peaks of the Crillin. There is a peculiar clearness and remoteness in a distant view to the north-west, whether by day, when the far horizon is sharp and the sky very cold and pure, or at night, when stars shine faintly through the shifting beams of the Aurora. It was some perception of this quality that made a friend of mine describe Coigeach as a "place fit only for disembodied spirits". At the bottom of the arable is a marshy tract of grazing, sweet with bog-myrtle, which reaches to the edge of the foreshore and is called the Lon Liath or hoary marsh, perhaps because there are so many grey rocks in it.

The second piece, on the far side of the hillock where Katie spreads her washing to bleach, lay at the head of a long narrow gully or "glac", which ran down to a rocky cove called Port nam Feannagan.* Though within hail of Sandy's house, it might have been miles from any human habitation. The outer rim of the hollow was sharp and steep and a low dyke ran along it, much as Hadrian's Wall skirts the Northumbrian crags. The brilliant green grass, starred in spring with golden kingcups and bluebells, the weathered stones of the dyke tufted with lichen, the Cuillin sharp against the sunset, and the surf moaning on the rocks gave to this place a unique beauty. I would not exchange it for any plot in the kingdom.

This ground, which yielded a short-stemmed but thick and sweet crop of hay, had once been a bog-myrtle scrub. The farther end, where the land dropped abruptly to shore level, was still covered with a miniature thicket of this shrub with a little bracken and heather and a few dwarf oaks no bigger than small bushes. At odd moments, when there was nothing better to do, I would go for a while and pull up the bog myrtle. It had spreading roots and suckers but they were near the surface and easily pulled. The fragrant oil from the crushed leaves made this quite a pleasant job. There was good grass growing in the scrub and I intended,

* Harbour of the Lazy-beds or perhaps of the hoodie crows. The Gaelic word is the same for either.

when the clearing was finished, to dress it heavily with dung and seaweed, reckoning that it would make a useful addition to my stock of hay. But later, when I acquired more land in the Goirtean, this little job was practically abandoned as not worth the labour, though I did go back to it on days which were too wet for digging but not wet enough to keep me indoors.

The third piece was a mere pocket handkerchief at the bottom of the gully, carefully marked with sticks in the spring to avoid mistakes. It was inclined to be wet and, lying under the rock and facing north, had little sun and poor drying. But all the same it gave me a useful coil of hay.

7

The Lon and the Blar Eorna

I. The Lon

THE rest of my croft was over the hill and far from home, on the eastern side of the pass. Part of it – rather more than an acre in all – lay in the Lon. This, as the name implies, was a marshy flat in a hollow of the hill, which the labour of ages had made into a green jewel set in a wild ring of rock and heather. It was enclosed by an ancient dyke, breached in many places, and anyhow too low to keep out the cattle, which were never suffered to go unherded. In this island of husbandry every crofter in Smirisary but Angus Ruairidh had a share. The land was divided into long narrow strips, intersected by drains that had bitten deep into the peaty soil, making the place dangerous for grazing beasts. The careful cultivation of generations – the turning with spades, the mowing with sickle and scythe, and the countless creels of dung and seaweed carried from byre and shore on the backs of men had forced this naturally sour, cold soil to yield abundant hay and excellent potatoes.

The Lon was far from all the homesteads and out of sight – a great drawback, though most of the crofters had to pass through it on their daily trip to the peat-banks and could see if anything were amiss. Also the carrying up of dung and seaweed and the carrying down of any crop that was grown there brought much toil to men without horses. Some people solved this problem by building their byres in the Lon itself, so that the dung was handy to the soil and the hay to the beasts. But every convenience has its snag – in this case the labour of going up twice daily in winter to feed the cattle. To me, a distant byre is a nightmare. My own, though discreetly facing away from the house, was so near that on still nights I could hear the cows munching and rattling their chains. True, I had some distance to go with the manure, but then I had a horse, which made all the difference.

I liked to see the Lon in early spring, when after the muck of winter all was dry and the naked hills and bleached, withered grass were veiled with smoke from heather fires, which drifted down from the Bairness on the steady east wind. The newly-turned potato ground lay black and smooth, without a stone, or a weed, or a bramble anywhere. On the grass plots were tidy rows of rich brown dung-heaps, among which men were moving with creels and graips, some spreading, others bringing loads from the byre middens, which they couped with a single deft movement. Round their bowed figures the pungent smoke eddied and rolled; and beyond, the early April sky, still cold and faintly blue, was loud with the passion of larks.

In August all was changed. The song of birds had ceased and anxious ewes were calling to lambs grown big and head-strong. The dung-heaps were replaced by equally neat rows of corn-stooks and coils of hay. The same men were at work, but now with scythes and rakes. The hill, so bare in spring, would be glowing with heather, wine-dark under the shadow of clouds. The drains were full of meadow-sweet and loosestrife and, instead of the harsh piping of wind and tang of smoke, came the murmur of wild bees and the drowsy scent of earth's fulness.

There is something in these scenes of immemorial labour that moves the heart as little else can do. Years ago, when I was only a spectator, I could never pass a thatched byre on a knollie, or men scything among the moon-daisies, or sheep being gathered from the hill, without a stirring of nostalgic emotion, as if in this I saw something I had always wanted and might be too late to find. But now that I am myself part of the life I looked at, the emotion has deepened into a settled content, for I know that the treasure is still there and has not been overvalued.

Everything in the Lon was very tidy; the byres were neatly thatched and the middens well-squared. But for some time the seemliness of the place had been marred by the derelict scrubby appearance of the vacant croft, which none of the neighbours had thought worth cultivating. There were indeed a few patches of grass that could still be mown, but even these were rapidly going back from lack of manure. The rest was a mass of rushes, handy enough for thatching or pitting potatoes but otherwise a useless eyesore. The drains were choked with rushes and brambles, and in places water was seeping onto the land.

By exchange with a neighbour, I got a continuous piece large enough to plough, though only in one direction as a wide drain down the middle prevented cross-ploughing. The rest of my plots were too small and broken up by drains for anything but spade cultivation. The first winter, I spent much time in cutting the rushes, gathering them into bundles, and carrying them to the side, where on a dry day in spring they were burned and the ashes scattered. Rush-cutting soon blunts a scythe, and at that time of the year there was no one about in the Lon who might have sharpened it; one rub by an expert was worth a dozen of my own. Also I let the point catch in a bramble root and broke it; and though Angus sorted it with a file, it never went through the rushes as it should, and the work was slow and laborious. I was curiously watched by herdsmen on the hill for a woman with a scythe was not a common sight. But the chief problem of work in the Lon was where and how to get meals. It was too far from the house to be for ever going back to light a fire and cook. In those days Annie would often give me tea, a kindness which I shall never forget.

I persuaded Donald, the estate shepherd and ploughman, to do the ploughing. I had a small "Landmark" plough, but this he scorned and we had a bad time getting his own full-sized implement to the scene of action. We brought it to the end of the road in a cart, whence it was half dragged, half carried over burns, bogs, and rocks to the boundary dyke of the Lon, where a gap was opened to let it through. The ploughing itself went well enough, the furrows lying straight and even, and I was just thinking that this job, unlike so many in the Highlands, was going to end without a hitch, when the grey horse's hames broke, and the few remaining furrows had to be left till the next day. Infinite patience, if not fatalistic acquiescence, is needed in anyone who does anything or, even more, who wishes anything done by others in this enchanting but exasperating country. So little does anything ever go according to plan, that it is far better to arrange nothing beforehand and trust to the inspiration of the moment. There is much talk of "planning" for the Highlands. Blessed word! You may indeed plan and in the end something may result; but it will not be the thing that was planned.

I remember an occasion, some years ago at Fernaig, when a young neighbour came to earth up the Laird's acre of potatoes. The drill plough was lying in the field but the sock was missing and had to be recovered from the person who had last borrowed it. The swingle-trees belonging to the plough were previously used on the chain harrows, to which, in default of hooks, they had been lashed with wire and lashed so securely that it took a long time to cut through the various knots and hitches. One of the horses had a loose shoe, the other was minus a back-band, and one set of chains was mislaid. The reins were missing but were eventually discovered in a stall in the byre. It took much longer to collect and repair things than to earth up the potatoes. But the Laird did not worry; thirty-five years in the West had taught him to swim with the stream.

Donald sowed the seed, while I harrowed it in with one horse and a single section of the harrows weighted with a big stone; the plot was too narrow for the full set. It gave me great satisfaction to see this derelict land under a crop; and when the corn was well up, I went along the road to Loch na Bairness and looked down on that square of brilliant green in its setting of rock and heather. Beside the corn was a narrow strip of ground, spoilt for ploughing by drains. This I devoted to potatoes, and dug it by hand, helped by Raymond O'Malley, a former schoolmaster who was working at Samalaman. We dug side by side, turning the sod in long rolls, as is the local custom. When a former proprietor reclaimed the Laran Mor, it was not ploughed but dug by a line of twelve men abreast; in those days wages were low, and the Laird was rich. I had the offer of dung from the MacNeils's midden, which was not far off, and with the help of Graham's pony and borrowed creels I shifted a number of loads. But if the distance was short, the path was incredibly rough and narrow and neither pony nor leader enjoyed it.

The Lon was swarming with rabbits and I decided to put a fence with wire netting round the corn. No larch stobs were to be had, so O'Malley and I cut birch posts in the woods – a poor expedient, for birch rots quickly, and in three years' time most of the posts were useless. We carted them to the end of the road and then carried them in bundles on our backs. The rolls of netting and coils of fencing wire were brought on horseback. Neither of us had erected a fence before and, all things considered, we did not make too bad a job of it.

The further history of the Lon must be kept for another chapter. A place snatched from the wild is always full of disappointments. Nature, so friendly-seeming when we do not interfere, can become an enemy strong, cunning, and merciless. This in itself is stimulating. The danger comes only when we are tired and the lions in the path are larger than life, roaring horribly; when the difficulties cease to be a challenge to our courage and resource, and become a burden too heavy to be borne. Luckily for me, having just enough to live on, I was able to slack off before the breaking-point.

II. The Blar Eorna

The other completely derelict piece of my croft was called the Blar Eorna. It lay north of the Lon and separated from it by a fold of the hill on which was a ruin still known as the Weaver's House (Tigh an Fhigheadair) though it was many years since the weaver died. It had once been good land: the name means Barley Field, and near it was a hillock called Cnoc a' Mhullain, or the Hillock of the Stack. In former times, there was no grass on the crofters' arable: every inch was turned and planted with potatoes or sown with corn, mostly barley which produced drink as well as food, for those were the days of illicit stills.

The Blar Eorna had been long out of cultivation and its appearance was daunting. It was cut in two by a small burn, whose course was choked with rushes, brambles, and dwarf willow, and the evil had spread to the open drains, which, as everywhere else on the estate, were far too numerous.

In the West Highlands, the sequence of land deterioration is always the same. When draining and manuring cease, the better and more nutritious grasses die out, giving place to Yorkshire fog, sorrel, and buttercup. Where hay has been the last crop, the turf becomes thick and matted, while potatoes leave behind them a mass of rank weeds. These, as the soil becomes more and more acid and water-logged, yield to tussock grass and rushes, which, by growing in thick clumps and mats, check drainage still further and create conditions increasingly favourable to themselves. Dwarf willow spreads along the banks of burns and in the bottoms of drains; its tangle of creeping roots, gathering the debris of spates, imprisons the surplus water and turns the place into a sour swamp which grazing animals avoid. Low ground that has been out of cultivation for thirty or forty years is covered by a dense forest of rushes, and the soil becomes so choked with layers of decay that no grass grows but only moss, lichens, and fungi. Untrampled by cattle or sheep, the mossy carpet is so thick that to cross it is like walking on a wet sponge.

The lower part of the Blar Eorna, when I first saw it, had nearly reached this stage, but the upper end was fairly clear of rushes and carried a thick but dirty crop of inferior grass, mainly Yorkshire fog. On the knollies, the herbage was better, but bracken and brambles were encroaching everywhere. During the first winter and spring I made a determined attack on this land. I cut the rushes three times with a scythe, cleared part of the willow scrub and brambles and, with O'Malley's assistance, cleaned out the lower course of the burn and some of the main drains, he cutting the sods and I lifting them with a "hawk" or bent graip. This was hard work, but the pleasure of freeing the imprisoned water and watching the drains run made it seem worth while. In draining, you see results more quickly and obviously than in almost any other kind of agricultural work. Then I gave the better grass a drastic harrowing, cut the bracken twice, put out as much dung (from a neighbour's midden) as I had time for and in May gave a dressing of sulphate of ammonia to all that was worth mowing. This last was a mistake. It certainly increased the first crop, but the following year there was hardly any grass. On a soil so lacking in lime, nitro-chalk would have been better, or perhaps no artificial at all. With true Oxford indecision, I am still swithering between the Compost School and orthodox farming practice. This year, my bag of nitro-chalk mysteriously disappeared from the Samalaman boathouse. Perhaps this was a sign; at any rate, I don't think I shall bother to order any more.

Some of the outlying grass was spoilt by rabbits and straying cattle but I secured two little stacks of hay. They were not of the best quality but made a useful addition to my store and in the following spring I even had a small surplus to sell.

That was the first crop of hay I took from the Blar Eorna, and it is likely to be the last. When, in my second season, I had livestock to look after and an ever-increasing garden to keep in order I found the derelict and outlying parts of the croft impossible to work single-handed. Had they been near the homestead and out of cultivation, or far away and in good heart, or even had I been able to reach them with a cart, I might have managed. But the rushes, the distance, the roadlessness, and my own lack of help indoors and out combined to defeat me. In 1944, I abandoned the Blar Eorna and concentrated on the land nearer home. In 1946, when I took over Sandy's croft in the Goirtean, I withdrew from the Lon also. But I still paid rent for both these pieces, hoping to exchange them at some future redistribution of holdings.

8

Winter Nights

IT was my misfortune to begin the Smirisary adventure in November, so that the first few months, always the worst in a new place, fell in the darkness of a stormy winter. I was not yet familiar with the technique of living, the special and local knowledge that everyone, however travelled and hardy, must acquire in order to be reasonably comfortable. It was not a cold winter but after that halcyon November we had nothing but rain and gales till spring, and the whole place was a sea of mud through which one ploughed, weary and heavy laden, with leaky gumboots. Every lump of coal and bit of peat, every stick, every drop of paraffin, every match even, had to be counted and considered. The shoddy inadequacy of war-time clothes and shoes is bad enough in town; on the wild hills of the north it becomes a minor tragedy. My feet were never dry, and I was for ever cobbling the gaping holes in my stockings with tags of wool begged from this friend or that.

At Samalaman, the Crolls were in a worse plight. They were newly arrived in a big draughty house, with hard beds and threadbare carpets taken over from the last owner. They had no coal, and though there was plenty of fuel in the woods, labour was lacking to cut it. Innumerable high windows had to be blacked out with every kind of emergency contraption and this routine wasted an hour or two morning and evening. The big old-fashioned range was impossible and at one time Mrs Croll, who had been reared in the lap of luxury, was on her knees cooking for a household of eight on the open fire in the dining-room, where the balancing of pans and kettles on crumbling and collapsing logs became a fine art. There was a general shortage of torch batteries and Aladdin lamp mantles, and a local shortage of paraffin, candles, and matches, the allowance for the Big House being half-a-gallon of oil, one candle, and one box of matches weekly. This, in the dead of winter in the far north, where daylight does not come till nearly ten and goes again before four, was a trial; it lowered morale. The first time – in February – that we could have tea without a light seemed worth treating as a festival.

Already, at Newton, I had known the race to get things done before dark; no one who has not worked on a farm in winter can fully appreciate the truth of "The night cometh, when no man can work". At Smirisary, though the span of daylight was less than in Cornwall, the press of work was not so great and there was no need for much artificial light in the morning. On the crofts, where little is done in winter but attending to beasts, carrying peats and cutting wood, it is not thought worth while to rise before daybreak, unless for some special ploy, and my usual hour of eight was considered very early.

Of recent years, especially since the war, the winter has seemed long to me. The first morning we rise by lamplight, the first night we give hay to the cows, bring a sense of loneliness, of abandonment, like that which comes when we watch the ebbing of light from the world on a stormy evening. Another dawn will come, another spring, but who will see it? Somewhere, sometime our hour lies in wait for us and time, consuming our days, sweeps each one nearer to his hidden end. The long nights in themselves must always be a strain, especially in bad weather, when there is neither moon nor stars to comfort. And the war years added the misery of the black-out, when the glen was a pit of darkness, without the swinging of lanterns or friendly squares of lighted windows. Few nights passed without the distant boom of heavy firing or the rattle of the Commandos' machine guns and searchlights with flares in the southern sky. Sometimes there would be the drone of an aeroplane, perhaps one of our own, perhaps not. I have never been afraid to sleep in a house alone, but at that time I began to feel a little desolate and would go to bed with my hurricane lamp on the floor beside me, turned very low, so as to save oil and also to avoid being seen by a wakeful neighbour, for I still had my pride!

There is more bad weather in winter, and it is more noticeable because much of it comes in the long night and is thus magnified. A small one-storeyed cottage by the sea with only one person in it, especially if it has a galvanised iron roof and is lighted by war-time lamps and candles, seems a very inadequate shelter in a storm. I never spent a night at Samalaman without being made aware of the security of a big house; the elements cease to dominate and one can think of something else.

I came to loathe my iron roof and to dread the nights of storm spent under it. The wind struck it stunning blows; a shower of rain sounded like hail and hailstones like machine gun bullets. There is much hail in the West Highlands – how much I did not realise until I slept under iron. The interaction between warm sea and cold land makes for instability, and the uprush of warm air that causes hail is sometimes strong enough to produce thunder as well. On the Atlantic coasts, thunderstorms are commoner in winter than in summer and come mostly in short, sharp squalls when, after a muggy period of southerly rain, the wind veers suddenly to the west.

In January 1943, in the small hours, came a storm that turned my dislike of the iron roof into horror. Since sunset it had blown hard from the south-west, with a heavy sea. At about two in the morning I woke from an uneasy doze to find that the wind had dropped and the silence was filled with the roaring of the surf. In a momentary lull between waves, I heard a sighing far up in the air, which passed over the house and died away. Then came a clap of wind, which increased till there was a great clamour; and after that, I was aware of something that was neither wind nor sea. Trembling with ancient fears, I fumbled for matches and lit the candle. The thin flame drew up, guttering in the draught and casting faint, wavering shadows. A moment later, the world outside dissolved in chaos: flash on flash, crash after crash, with wind in a screaming crescendo; and then, drowning all else, a bombardment of hailstones on ninety-six square yards of galvanised iron. This lasted about ten minutes and then stopped as suddenly as it had begun. There was an awful hush, filled only by the solemn booming of the surf.

It was not long before the Crolls discovered this phobia of mine and I had a standing invitation to spend the night at Samalaman whenever the weather promised to be really dirty. On such occasions, I would have my tea, milk and feed the cows, and then take flight, returning early in the morning to milk and feed as usual.

On a wild night, the byre was even noisier than the house. It was a little nearer the sea; the galvanised roof was unlined, and the wind whistled through a thousand chinks in the drystone walls. The crash of waves on the Seann Rudha and the drumming of rain on iron drowned the steady ping of milk in the pail and the comfortable rumblings in the cows' bellies. Yet to the eye the scene was homely and secure. The lantern burned serenely on a ledge above the stalls, casting a warm light on the backs of the cows, stolidly munching their hay, and on the friendly miscellaneous junk that gathers in such a place – bundles of bracken, graips and shovels, old boxes and tins under the roof, a scythe hanging from the couples, a string of home-grown onions. Milking over, I would throw the beasts some more hay, bed them down and secure all doors; and then, taking a torch and knapsack, watch for a lull between squalls, and flee up the brae. If, when emerging from the house, I could still see the lights on Eigg and Bo Fhaskadail, I would have time to reach the leeward side of the pass and drop into the hollow of Allt Ruadh before the next squall caught me. People wondered how I could go out in such weather. But the wildness made me restless, and I would rather move than sit still and wait for what might be coming. At the top of the brae, I would glance behind me to see if the lights were still clear. Often they had vanished, lost in a moving curtain of rain. Away to the north, above a bank of clouds on which lightning played, was an arch of greenish sky, with a few tremulous stars, soon to be quenched. If there was thunder afar, the noise of the surf drowned it; and round the Seann Rudha was a white turmoil of foam lit by an unearthly sheen that came from nowhere. Sandy Gillies once said – and I noticed it myself – that a really dirty night is rarely dark. There seems to be a phosphorescence in the air, like that described by Victor Hugo in *Travailleurs de la Mer*.

I gained the pass, and dropped below it into comparative calm, where I could hear the gale pouring over the ridge above and behind me. At the gate, which was farther from the sheltering hill, there was a demoniac shrieking in the wires of the march fence as the squall overtook me. Pulling down my hat to protect my ears from the hail, I ran on in a hissing whitish mist, until the roaring of the big beeches and firs round Samalaman told me I was nearly at my destination. As I burst into the kitchen, a scurry of wind followed me, with which I wrestled to close the door. Later, playing bridge or luxuriating in a hot bath, the tumult I had left seemed no more than a bad dream.

It was the roof that played on my nerves – the cheap, easily-laid, ugly, and in every way unsatisfactory galvanised iron, cold in winter, hot in summer and infernal in a storm. The old Highland houses may have been dirty and insanitary, but their builders knew the climate and the supreme need for shelter. The three-foot-thick stone walls were rounded at the corners, and the roof, thatched with heather or rushes secured with ropes or netting, was blunt ended, so that the whole house was streamlined and offered the least possible resistance to the wind. To go inside was like entering a cave, full of warmth, shelter, and silence. Compare with this the thin concrete walls, iron or asbestos roofs and ill-fitting windows of the modern croft house, which even in the most exposed islands is rapidly replacing the indigenous dwellings. I resolved to alter my roof but it was some time before I could do so and meanwhile I was comforted to find that Sandy Gillies, who also slept under galvanised iron, disliked it as much as I did. After each stormy night he vowed that he would flit; and on the morrow of a particularly violent gale, said that he had not gone to bed at all and would rather be a tramp on the roads than spend another winter at the Goirtean.

But there were not many really dirty nights and they were fully compensated by the exquisite beauty of the good ones. Nights of serene moonlight, when I would go late to the well, over grass crackling faintly with frost, still showing the scythe-marks; and by the burn, the lovely rustling ghosts of last summer's cow-parsley, its umbels still perfect in desiccation. On such nights, I would be in no hurry to take in the pony. As I moved towards her, she would turn, whinnying softly; and the moon, swimming clear of Cnoc O Leo, would turn her shaggy grey-white coat to silver and gleam on the links of the tether chain, worn bright with trailing over the ground. The peat smoke from Alan's house would rise and spread in the windless air, transparent and faintly gleaming like the substance of Ossian's ghosts, whose forms the stars shone through. The moon, piercing through ancient nail-holes in the byre roof, made discs of light within, as if there were silver sequins on the cows' backs. Conversely, if the night were dark and a lantern within, the holes (from outside) looked like stars painted on a back-cloth.

I remember also a calm night in November, when I was on my way home from the Goirtean. Being in no hurry to go inside, I stood for a while on Cnoc an t-Sabhail. This little eminence, though only about sixty feet above sea-level, was a fine vantage point from which you could look southward to Ardnamurchan light and away beyond Skye to the mysterious north. Here the dark sky with its myriad frosty stars paled gradually towards the horizon; and I saw a rosy arch, reaching from Rhum to the hills of Morar, from which faint searchlight gleams pulsed and shifted, now brightening, now fading; and in the midst, like a brooch set in a floating veil, the Pole star shone. Beneath, Rhu Arisaig lay very still and the intervening sea was touched with auroral light and gleamed faintly like pewter in candlelight. A slight swell was rolling in and the waters, divided by the promontory of the Faing Mor, sighed in antiphony, with a deeper note round the Seann Rudha and more softly on the rocks that fringed Port nam Feannagan and the Lon Liath. At last, when it became too cold to linger, I turned home, past the byre with its comfortable munching, to fire and lamplight and a warm bed.

Sometimes I would spend the evening at Tigh Ruairidh, as the MacPhersons' house was called, Ruairidh (Roderick) being the name of their father. I had a bundle of stockings to darn, while Annie knitted, and Angus turned over old papers or talked, for he had no indoor hobby. The kitchen, always spotlessly clean and tidy, was arranged on the traditional plan. The long wall facing the window was occupied by two box beds with gathered curtains, which turned them into cubicles so that people of different sexes could have privacy and yet enjoy the only fire. There were no easy chairs, and the beds could be used to rest upon during the day. Each had a crucifix and a holy picture at its head. There was also a table, a dresser full of dishes, two or three wooden chairs, and a long bench under the window. Such benches and dressers would often be made by the joiner in the room they were to occupy, as the doors were too narrow to admit the finished article. In Tigh Ruairidh, built only some forty years ago to replace an older dwelling, now a barn, the fire was no longer on the hearth, but in an iron grate with an oven at the side. This last was hardly ever used for Annie did all her baking on the girdle.

We always spoke in Gaelic. Annie had fluent English, for she had been in service in Glasgow before coming home to keep house for her brother, but long years in Smirisary, where it was needed only for the visiting gentry, had made her less ready with the fashionable tongue. And Angus, though he could understand English and speak it slowly, preferred bad Gaelic to none at all. Sometimes I would persuade them to sing, though they would never get going unless I sang first. Some of their songs were those well known all over the Highlands, others were unpublished local efforts, for in the not very distant past people still extemporised on the doings of their neighbours. There was a boat song, with a great many verses, about the lads of Smirisary, but the only person who could produce more than one verse was a policeman in Glasgow, whose visit was too short for me to get a complete version written down. The satire, a form much enjoyed by the older Gaels and a sound alternative to malicious gossip, was still remembered here, though I think not practised, and its counterpart, the eulogy, was not unknown. When Graham Croll was farming in Morvern, a woman from Harris, who was settled in the district, made a song in his praise which was sung at a *ceilidh* held in his own barn.

Once, at a *ceilidh* in my own house, Angus recited one of the traditional tales he had learned as a boy from Charlie MacPherson, a great story-teller who lived in the lower house (now a ruin) in the Goirtean. It was a long story, called "*Mac Righ na Cathair Shiomain agus Nighean Og an Fhomhair Mhoir,*" (The Son of the King of the Straw Chair and The Young Daughter of the Giant) and took fully half-an-hour to recite. Like the Homeric poems, these tales contain many repetitions to aid the memory, some of them being archaic phrases, often strings of adjectives, in the old bardic style, which are not always understood: the people call them *Gaidhlig Dhomhain* or deep Gaelic. Some of the incidents I had already met with in Campbell's *West Highland Tales,* but much of the story was new to me, especially the last part, which may be a Catholic variant for it contains three comic ministers. Later, I persuaded him to tell it again slowly and I succeeded in getting it written down.

Very few of the older people, and not a great many of the younger ones, could read and write their native tongue. Thus, I was sometimes asked to read aloud stories from the few Gaelic books I possessed, or the Gaelic page provided by some of the local weekly papers. This must have been poor entertainment, for I read with a strong English accent and stumbled over the less familiar words – a failing that Annie politely blamed upon the dimness of her lamp. That was before I gave them an Aladdin – I don't know what she will find to say now. At the Goirtean, Gaelic readings were not needed, for Sandy and his younger daughter were both good readers. Moreover, there was a wireless and a number of young children, all in the same room.

In Glenuig, far from the blighting influence of Calvinism, the winter was enlivened with many dances and *ceilidhs*, or a combination of the two, for songs were interspersed between vigorous reels to rest the dancers and give the older people an innings. Apart from an occasional waltz, the dances were all Highland, with fiddle or pipes for music. The singers, who always sang in Gaelic, stood up simply, without accompaniment, and everyone joined in the choruses. If they were nervous, they did not show it, though someone might pitch the first verse too high or too low and then, being skied or grounded, would cheerfully continue in another key. But long or short, good or bad, every song was received with loud applause.

For many years past, the Russian Benedictine, Father Cyril Dieckhoff, who was a fine Gaelic scholar, had been coming from Fort Augustus Abbey to Glenuig at Christmas time to collect songs and stories and hold a big *ceilidh* in the schoolroom. He was a delightful old man and his love for the people, and theirs for him, made everything go with a swing, in spite of the heat and the over-narrow benches on which we were packed like sardines.

Before we leave the Glenuig schoolroom, here is a tale of false teeth; and the tragedy of false teeth is that they are intensely serious, and yet no one can take them seriously.

71

Everyone laughs at dentures; and yet to have them is an embarrassment, to lose them a disaster, and even worse to share them, like the couple I knew in Ross-shire, who could never go out together, because they had only one set.

A month or two after my arrival at Smirisary there was a dance in the schoolroom, to which Mrs Croll and I went together. As usual, the room was very hot and, after awhile feeling a little squeamish, I slipped out into the cold air, and in a dark corner of the schoolhouse enclosure was violently sick. Mrs Croll, thinking something amiss, followed me out and took me to Maisie's house, where Father Bradley gave me some whisky. Revived by the dram, I was conscious of a loss. "My God, my teeth!" I exclaimed. "I'll go and look for them", said Mrs Croll soothingly. "You will not!" I protested bleakly imagining her groping with a torch among the dockens of the school yard, and almost certainly in vain, for it was hard to explain exactly where I had lost them, and the plate was very small. "No, I'll go myself", I continued, staggering to my feet; "I must !" How could the Lady of Glenuig, so newly arrived herself, be seen – for seen she would be – doing something so menial, so ridiculous, as searching the ground for someone else's teeth? Ignoring her protests, I doddered back to the schoolhouse. Light streamed from the open door, where a group of young fellows were cooling themselves between dances. I thought that by dousing my torch and slipping round the side in the shadow, I might avoid detection. But then a dog heard me and barked. I could not face it and fled back, intending to return in the morning. This Mrs Croll would not hear of, and, settling me firmly in an armchair, she walked over to the school. When the opening of another dance had drawn the lads inside, she searched in the place indicated and at last returned in triumph with the lost treasure wrapped in a handkerchief.

Small impromptu *ceilidhs* were often arranged at the Big House, especially when there were musical visitors, who might themselves be willing to perform, or be interested to hear a few Gaelic songs. One of these *ceilidhs* fell on a night in February. Even before I left home, a few flakes were falling and, by the time the music was over, the southeasterly wind had risen to a gale and the snow was thicker and beginning to drift. I did not return to Smirisary that night and when I woke in the morning the irregularities of the ground were planed smooth and the gates in the steading drifted up to the top, though the wind had shifted to the south-west and a thaw had set in. After breakfast I started on the way home and was delayed in places by drifts several feet deep, which were beginning to get soft on top. On reaching the house, I found a hard-packed mass of snow between the midden and the byre wall, which completely blocked the door. Luckily the spade, which I usually kept in the byre, was in the lobby of the house and I was able to dig a way to the cows. Inside, to my complete astonishment, a layer of snow covered everything but the beasts themselves and the floor near them, where the warmth of their bodies had melted the flakes as they fell. The gale had driven the snow, which was very fine and powdery, clean through the chinks of the drystone walls and through the star-like nail holes in the roof. As I milked, I heard on all sides the sound of running water, and the mugginess of the air warned me that if I did not hasten to clear the drift at the byre door it would dam back the melting snow water and flood the whole place. I worked feverishly with the spade until I had it cleared, and none too soon. The thaw was in full swing, the temperature having risen ten degrees in a very few hours. Every burn was in spate, every ditch and drain overflowing. Water poured down the brae at the back of the house; the path became a torrent and, when the flood subsided, looked more like a furrowed scree than a road. The big drifts on the pass, having been in the track of the blizzard and packed hard, took two or three days to go and no one but myself attempted to clear them. The others patiently waited for the Power that sent the snow to remove it.

9

Spring Work

FOR mud, storm, and darkness there was little to choose between December and January; only, in the first month of the year, we had rounded the Horn, and the days were noticeably lengthening. At Smirisary, the return of the light had not the same urgency as at Fernaig, where the high southern hills shadowed the glen from the end of November till the middle of January. With our open horizon, we never lost the sun and, on clear days, the house basked in sunshine from dinner-time till dusk. In February, the pace quickened. On mild days, you might perceive a faint stirring of life, as if the brown, desiccated land were turning in its sleep. Yet, as crofters, we were entering upon the hardest period of the winter. It is said that in the middle of February a good husbandman should have half his winter keep untouched in the barn. The grass of the crofts was grazed bare, the heather and bents of the hill were dun and bleached, and beasts that looked fat enough at Christmas were rapidly losing condition. In the old days, before the technique of winter feeding was properly understood, many animals died in the lean months, and the emaciated survivors would stagger from the byres and stand blinking in the merciless spring sunshine. Some were too weak to walk and had to be carried bodily to pasture. Many a Highland cow, like the hinds whose privations they shared, would calve only once in two years. The crofters themselves were often in no better case. Not seldom, especially in the islands, stores of potatoes and grain would run out and people be forced to gather shell-fish and edible seaweed. Thanks to modern transport, these hardships have gone; shell-fish are still gathered, but for the London market. Yet even now, in remote and inaccessible places, snowdrifts or frozen lochs or heavy seas may for a season bring them back. As late as 1900, the schoolmaster in the Island of Scarp, off the West coast of Harris, wrote in his log: "No scholars to-day, as owing to food shortage, parents thought it advisable to keep the children in bed."

A shadow of the old spring famine survived in the late winter and spring shortage of milk. To economise wintering and to secure the best calves at the most favourable time, the majority of crofters' cows calved in late spring and early summer and started milking in the first flush of young grass. When autumn came and the yield began to decline, it was stimulated by the aftermath of hay. By the end of November this too had vanished and the scanty grazing of the hill was supplemented by hay, with perhaps a few sheaves or turnips fed in the byre. Cake and other purchased feeding stuffs were kept for stirks intended for the spring sales. Thus butter-making would cease before Christmas and by mid-January most cows were dry. Only here and there did anyone keep an autumn- or a winter-calving cow. They were expensive to winter, since one must keep them in a good deal, with concentrates, oatmeal drinks, and quantities of good hay. So people resigned themselves and bought condensed milk when obtainable, or just did without. It was a comfort that the egg shortage, which spoiled the autumn, did not coincide with the milk famine which spoiled the spring.

How deeply we cherished those first shy intimations of the chaste northern spring! I remember that day in early March when I went to the ravine of the Allt Ruadh to cut hazel rods for the new pony-creels which Angus Ruairidh was going to make for me – a day of soft skies and faint drifting showers, and a silky swell that moaned on the rocks of Lon Liath. I sauntered along the shore, past the cave where Sandy stored his bracken, and over the saw-tooth ridges of Rudha nan Iasgairean to Poll Beag. Here, on a level green half-ringed by cliff, was the long-abandoned ruin of a house with its byre and barn. The bed of the Allt

Ruadh burn, which here flowed north to seek the sea, was wide and shallow at its mouth, but deeply eroded above where the rush of water had carved a steep-sided ravine. The rocky braes sheltered a thicket of hazel, birch, and rowan with a dense undergrowth of heather, bramble, and honeysuckle. Perched on the limb of an ancient birch tree, which jutted across the gorge like the segment of a broken bridge, a black billy-goat of villainous aspect was browsing on the swelling buds. Here and there, the rich damp soil beneath the trees was starred with primroses and as I fought my way to the heart of the thicket my eyes and hands were delighted with the seductive dangle of hazel catkins and the silvery softness of pussy willows. There I found gleaming rods of hazel, springing in clumps from the old wood. I cut them with pruning secateurs and bound them into bundles with withies of honeysuckle. The bramble suckers, some eight or nine feet long, tripped me at every step, and soon my clothes were torn and my hands bleeding. The honeysuckle, too, was immensely tough and clung with a drowning man's grip to the rocks from whose crevices it sprang. But I managed to secure a piece with a root to transplant to the garden. It now flowers by the leaning gatepost, scenting the air as we come from the byre at the day's ending.

I was some time cutting enough rods for a pair of creels: it is surprising how many are needed, and how few, even in a good thicket, are really suitable. Angus, like all experts, would doubtless find fault with those I had chosen, but they would be duly peeled and stored in a shed to mature. Later, on a fine warm day, he would set up the stronger rods in an oval ring on the grass, the ends being stuck firmly in the ground; and then, with these as a foundation, he would begin to weave the creel. The usual type of peat creel is very light, having bands of open-work alternating with close weaving. It is excellent for a man carrying peats on his back but too light for a pony or for heavy loads of coal.

From the time of the bracken-cutting in October to the putting out of dung for potatoes in March, most of my neighbours spent their winter in semi-hibernation. Cattle indeed must be attended to, but they were let out late and brought home early, with a very long interval between the evening and the morning milking. Those who felt inclined might go winkle-gathering, or do a bit of fishing; others would cut a little firewood or clean out drains. A few, if their middens were beginning to block the byre door, might carry a creel or two of dung each day to the potato ground, where it would remain in a heap until the time of planting.

But I myself was forced to be more active for not only was I single-handed, but also slower and weaker than my neighbours and dreaded leaving too much till the spring. Then, too, I had a vegetable and flower garden, which needed clearing up in the autumn and digging and liming in winter. Any improvements or additions, such as wall-building, fencing, bramble-cutting, drainage, or the clearing of derelict corner, I liked to do between the middle of October and Christmas, so that the latter part of the winter and the early spring could be given to the more serious business of digging and dunging. In November and December the days were so short that I tried to have all the routine chores finished early, so that I could work on without interruption till dark and then go straight in to light the fire and the lamps and get myself tea.

The manuring was the year's heaviest work on the crofts. There is an amusing poem by Johnny Campbell, a South Uist crofter, called "*An t-innearadh's an racadh*" (The manuring and the raking) in which he says that, bad as the raking is, the manuring is far worse and advises all wise men to get a pony – and, he might have added, a cart. This, owing to rocks and drains innumerable, was not possible in Smirisary and the crofters used either creels or wheelbarrows. Both involved heavy work but, of the two, I would prefer the creel for, once you have learnt the knack of protecting yourself from the dirt and of heaving the creel on to your back, it was more easily managed on the soft uneven ground about the byres and could be instantly couped where required. The barrows were of the old-fashioned heavy wooden type, with iron tyres, and unless one's byre was above the field level and the ground really hard and sloping, this work was killing. Those with a large croft, like Angus Ruairidh, might have a byre at either end, so that the dung could more easily be put out. But what you saved in harrowing was lost in walking to and fro to milk and feed.

My neighbours used dung with plenty of bracken for potatoes, but preferred it neat for grass, as thus it was easier spread. The potato dung might go out in March, but most of the grassland was manured in April, or even in May, when the coating of muck on the young grass was thought to discourage marauding cows and sheep. In the old cattle-folding days, seaweed alone was used, and Angus Ruairidh claimed to be the first to put dung on the land. When I first came, Sandy Gillies was still cutting bladder-wrack on the rocks of the Lon Liath and carrying it in creels on his back to the Lon – a good half mile, and all uphill. About half-way up was a little green with a cairn of stones in the middle, round which the seaweed was dumped in heaps to dry and lose weight before being carried further. He said it was hard work for one man alone, morally as well as physically, and he began to reclaim some derelict land above the Lon Liath to which, little by little, he transferred his potatoes and manured them with dung from the byre above. In the Lon, he had grown excellent crops with half-rotted seaweed and a little compound potato fertiliser, which Gaelic speakers insist on calling "guano"! Presumably guano was the first imported manure known in these parts.

When Sandy ceased from cutting the wrack, he had no successor; but some use was still made of the masses of tangleweed cast up on the shore by storms and spring tides, which in Gaelic is called *bruchd*. The MacNeils carried up countless creels of it for their grass-land. With two able-bodied men heavily laden, the work was soon done, for the lower part of their croft was not far from the shore. The weed came in most plentifully in April, though sometimes, if the weather were unusually calm, it might fail to appear, or else come by stealth with the flood and go out with the following ebb before anyone had time to gather it. A heavy dressing of *bruchd* was considered a cure for rushes, and a very thick layer, applied in autumn and left to rot on the ground, would make tough old turf more amenable to the spade. This I tried with success, and also found that a compost of dung, tangle, sand, and annual weeds was excellent in the garden. The great disadvantages of *bruchd* was its appalling slipperiness and the difficulty of handling the heavy whiplike stems. Bladder wrack was easier to gather and, being fixed to the rocks, could be obtained at any ebb tide, but the cutting was laborious and needed some skill.

But whatever they do with seaweed now is not to be compared with the old days, when the big fishing boats came in laden with the precious stuff and everyone, women and all, waded out with creels to help unload, sometimes waist deep in the surf; there were no Wellingtons then, and no one minded a wetting. And soon, with much chaff and laughter, they would disperse in all directions over the land, and come back again for more, till the boats were empty.

My own manuring (except in the garden, where I used a barrow) was all done with the pony. At first I had creels slung on the hooks of the pack-saddle, but these, though easy to fill, were the devil and all to unload, for they held nearly a hundredweight of dung each and were too heavy to lift from the hooks unaided. Also the continual loading and unloading was straining them out of shape. So I lay awake at night, trying to devise some container that could be emptied without removing it from the saddle. In parts of Ireland, they make creels with hinged bottoms, which, on the sliding of a pin, dump the load where required. These would be hard to weave without experience; so I set to work on a pair of wooden slatted boxes, with the outer side hinged like a door, from which, as from a cart, the dung could be forked. They were strengthened at the corners with iron angle-plates and, at first, had iron hinges and hooks for fastening; but these were soon twisted out of shape and I replaced them with cord, which worked much better. The making of these boxes excited much interest, for my neighbours were not used to women joiners.

When working alone, I would back the pony against the dung-heap and then stand on the top and fling large forkfuls into each box alternately. This needed some dexterity, and sometimes a blob of muck would overshoot the mark and land on the patient brute's head or, falling short, bespatter her rump.

When Angus was with me, he did the loading and unloading, while I had nothing to do but lead the pony. On a fine day – and there are many such in the spring – it was good to be pottering to and fro over the faintly greening grass, in the sharp wind and bright sunshine, and see snow on distant hills and white horses on the dark-blue sea, and hear the jobble of steep little waves on the shore, and the song of larks far up in the sky. Sometimes there would be black-backed gulls sailing and swooping, and the shadow of their wings would fall on us, bringing a fleeting chill.

In the north, April is almost a winter month, with cutting winds and snow on the high tops. The arable ground is black and naked, the pasture bleached to bareness, the cattle shaggy and lean. Yet the days are long and ever lengthening, with a peculiar translucency, which gives to the stark hills, the faraway snows, and sharply cut horizons, a quality not of this world. The virginal youngness of all things pierces the heart: green spears of corn and new grass, primroses starring the edge of the burn, the frail cry of an early lamb, the blare of a calf from somebody's byre. They say that autumn is melancholy; but far more poignant is the song of a mavis heard in the cold April twilight, or the sight of daffodils waving their gallant banners in the snow.

I always enjoyed the spring work. My heart was full of

hope, without shadow of disappointment, and my head full of plans not yet frustrated. Everything was to be better than last year, every crop a record, with no thought of the cattle, deer, rabbits, birds, leather-jackets, and slugs in wait to destroy them. The cows would calve at the right time, and the garden-seeds be sown at the right intervals; everyone would keep the gates shut and no one would use (or even suggest using) the hay tripods for firewood. In the cool invigorating air, without mugginess or midges, I worked in spacious content, unthreatened by the invading dark. It was pleasant to see the ground clean, and to know that it would remain so for quite a long time: and pleasant to watch the crofts, so deserted in winter, spring to life in a moment, with a running to and fro with creels, and furious labour with spades.

The potato-planting was the centre of the crofters' spring work. Each man had a number of long narrow plots divided by deep drains and grass verges. The drains were a nuisance, for one was apt to fall into them, and the verges, though needed to keep the soil from sliding into the ditch, harboured weeds and slugs. Many people let the grass on them grow long and cut it for hay; but this I could never bring myself to do, partly because the cut grass always slipped into the drain, but far more because, having learned my job on a larger holding, I could never take the verges very seriously. The plots were not dug until the actual day of planting, when two men would work together, filling alternate trenches with dung from a heap at the side and laying on it the plump, pinkish seed, which was covered with soil from the next trench. The rows, running across the plot were very short but there were a great many of them. Each crofter would grow enough for his own household – and potatoes, being a staple food, were used without stint – and to feed stirks and hens, with perhaps a surplus for sale. The quality was always excellent. No one bothered with earlies; Kerr's Pink, which is immune and very tolerant of acidity, was the favourite maincrop variety.

The women were out, too, and any relation who could be induced to pay a visit at that season. Annie's elder brother, Iain Mor, who had once been a shepherd and now lived with a married sister at Shielfoot, invariably turned up to help with the potatoes. He would walk by the hill, taking the tidal ford across Loch Moidart from Eilean Shona; and he never sent word of his coming, or brought with him anything in the way of rations. Every so often, Annie, as if warned by some special sense, would say, "I think Iain Mor may come this week", and would air his bedding and bake some extra scones. Though over eighty, he walked like a man in his prime and could dig and scythe with the best of them. His arrival, if unexpected, could not go long unmarked, for he had a powerful, resonant voice which echoed all over the glen. He was a glutton for work and often annoyed the Tigh Ruairidh household by his love of early rising.

My own potatoes were on a smaller scale, as I had only myself to feed and kept no hens or stirks. There were a few rows of earlies from sprouted seed in the garden and one plot of Redskins on the croft. About four weeks after planting, before the sprouts appeared, we cleaned the rows with a rake, an operation which corresponds to the harrowing given by farmers to their crop. (It will be understood that most of the Smirisary plots were too narrow and too much cut up by drains for horses to work, even had the people possessed any.) Later, we hoed them two or three times, until the shaws, meeting across the rows, stifled any further growth of weeds.

In former times, when the crofter population was much larger and mainly dependent on local supplies of food, every square yard not planted with potatoes was devoted to oats or barley. Depopulation, imported foodstuffs, the prohibition of poteen-making and, as some think, the increasing wetness of the summers have banished grain from many of the townships and lessened it in all. Permanent meadow, often dirty and half-wild, has taken its place: grass-land, especially the poorer kind, requires less labour and will tolerate much moisture. When I first came to Smirisary, no corn had been grown there for a very long time, so that there was no crop to rotate with potatoes. Grass-seeds were rarely sown; the usual practice was to plant potatoes on the same land for several years in succession, with the aid of very heavy manuring, until the yield diminished, when the ground was "let out", or allowed to tumble down to grass. Such plots did indeed produce grass of a kind, for in so moist a climate, grass will come anywhere, on a thatched roof, on a wall, on your very doorstep; but with it came the foulest of weeds. On derelict land, it was easy to distinguish plots under permanent grass from those in which potatoes had been the last crop taken, for the latter was always overrun with dockens, sorrel, and buttercup.

During the last few years, I and most of my neighbours sowed a small quantity of oats. The sheaves could be threshed with a stick for the hens and the straw fed to cattle in November and December. For this crop, on plots too narrow for the plough, the ground could be turned with the spade in a quick, wholesale way, merely reversing the clod, sowing the seed, and raking it in. I enjoyed this digging; it was a peaceful, steady occupation, showing immediate results and allowing freedom of thought. Years of outdoor life had made me hardy, and I never had a sore back, though much of the digging would have been considered tough by gardeners. Nothing is more delightful than the sight of vivid green spears of young corn pricking through the dark soil; and pleasant too the thought that nothing more need be done till harvest.

I have already mentioned the corn in the Lon. The second year was unlucky. The Crolls, delayed by bad weather and other misfortunes, were far behind with their own work and Donald was unable to plough for me. There was no one else to be had and, being most unwilling to let the land go back after all the labours of the previous year, I resolved to do the job myself, though ploughing was a thing I had always left to the experts. But now there was no expert and I had the little "Landmark" one-horse plough, which I had once tried at Fernaig. But then I was on smooth level ground, with a sober, experienced Clydesdale mare, and the Laird to help and demonstrate. Now I had stiff, rough ground, and a horse that walked too fast for me; and I had to set the plough by the light of nature, with no one less ignorant than myself to help or advise. I persuaded a neighbour to lead the horse, so that I could give my undivided attention to the plough. In spite of this, the wretched implement, for reasons unguessed, kept nosing into the last furrow and I had to throw my whole weight on the left-hand stilt in an endeavour to keep straight. Whenever we reached a specially rough piece, the horse began to rush and the sock rose out of the ground, and I was dragged helpless at the tail. Somehow I got it finished; but the land looked like a rough sea turned to stone, or pressure ridges on a glacier. Later, I tried to mend matters by repeated harrowing; but the central drain made cross-harrowing impossible. Actually I worked the ground too fine; the seed was not sufficiently buried, and the birds had a good deal of it.

10

Blossom

As already stated, I was firmly resolved not to cumber myself with livestock the first winter, when I had no home-grown hay to give them and but little time to spend on their needs. An undisturbed six months, in which I could improve the place and learn the technique of living there, would be worth the passing annoyance of little milk and no transport of my own. However, in February I bought a puppy, less for work, I admit, than for company. Turning over the *Highland News*, I saw an advertisement from a shepherd in Knoydart, offering two black and white Bear-die collie pups. They were not far away – Knoydart is across Loch Nevis from Mallaig – and cheap. I sent for one.

On the day arranged, I went up to Lochailort and took the box from the station to the hotel, where I was to have lunch. As I opened the lid, there emerged a fluffy ball with bright scared eyes and a face like a black and white chrysanthemum or cactus dahlia. It fled under the sideboard and when I put in my hand to draw it out feebly attempted to bite. I kept it on my lap as I ate, feeding it with morsels until its long plumy tail began to beat faintly on my knee. The shepherd had kept the puppies in a shed with their mother and they had never been handled by man.

Then, to my disgust, I heard that the store-boat had gone: I had not yet learned that it never waited for the Mallaig train. Thus I was faced with a nine-mile tramp, carrying the pup which was too young to walk; and having expected to return by boat, my clothes were too heavy and shoes too thin for the rigours of the Bealach Breac. Long before I reached Roshven, I wished the wretched pup at the bottom of the sea. Now I carried it under one arm, now under the other, now in both like a baby, or again over my shoulder like a lamb; but, no matter how, it seemed to get larger and heavier at every step, and more and more awkward to hold, like the flamingo at the Queen's croquet party. I set it on its flat fluffy feet to see if it would walk a little way, but it merely sat down and looked at me. Cursing, I picked it up and plodded on. When I staggered into the Big House to rest and show my acquisition to the Crolls, Miss Knocker remarked, "Why, it's more like a flower than a puppy!" Perhaps – but I was tired. I called her Dileas, after one of the old Fernaig dogs long since dead. The name means faithful, the Gaelic equivalent for "Fido". She had never been much use for work but was, and is still, a good companion.

A pony to save my back was the prime need. I knew it would be hard to get what I wanted – a quiet, good-tempered beast, and above all sure-footed and easy to catch. I had always admired the dun Barra ponies, which I had seen roaming in herds on the *machair* of Allasdale. In May I wrote to one of my crofter acquaintances, who made a business of breeding and selling ponies. He offered me a dun gelding, four years old and newly broken. At that time, the Outer Islands were still a forbidden area and it was impossible for me to look for myself. The answers to my very detailed enquiries were satisfactory and at last I decided to take the pony.

Michael, as I called him – it is a common name in Barra – arrived and was taken home more easily than Dileas. He was a bonny beast to look at – golden brown with black points, stocky, and as surefooted as a goat. He seemed quiet as well, though showing the whites of his eyes too much for my taste. Summer was on its way, with plenty of grass; and we arranged to put Michael into Poll Beag at night, with Dolly, the Allt Ruadh pony, for company. Then I discovered the snag. Michael was not only difficult to catch – many ponies are, especially on young grass – but he was wicked as well. He would come meekly enough to a pail of corn, and then, when you put out your hand, would rear

suddenly and box with his forefeet – a dangerous habit, and difficult to break. I did not feel like coping with this for, having never handled horses in youth, I was without the capacity, or even the ambition, to manage a tough customer. So I rid myself of Michael and set about looking for another.

I could get nothing locally, and at last wrote to the salesman at Fort William, who used to tour the Hebrides in search of horses and cattle, giving a detailed list of requirements. Six weeks later he wired me to expect a pony on the goods train next day. The train was late; and waiting on the platform I was consumed with every kind of misgiving, for I had never, before Michael, bought a horse without seeing it. The pony had been through the sale-ring, where it made a price which I, not knowing the beast, would never have offered. So it was just as well I left it to the salesman, for now, after four years' service and companionship, I would not take three times the price I paid.

The train came in at last, with a cattle-truck at the rear. On entering, I had a slight shock of disappointment. The pony was from Ormiclete in South Uist, and somehow I had expected a dun; but what I saw was a white mare, faintly dappled with grey. Not knowing her former name, I called her Blossom: it is a good farm-horse name, and suited her colour. At Ormiclete she was probably Bessie or Star. The Gaelic-speaking Highlander hardly ever gives his animals Gaelic names; that is left to Sassanachs and other fancy people. Dogs are Lassie or Dick or Sweep: cows may be Daisy or Maggie, but as often as not, have no name at all, being known as the Big One or the Black One, which sometimes leads to confusion. To call cows after one's friends, as I often did, seemed to shock people a little, though the crofters make great pets of their cattle. For years there had been no horses in Smirisary and, as long as there were plenty of able-bodied people to shoulder the burdens, their help was not greatly needed. The arable plots were mostly too small for the plough, there was no road fit for wheels, and a horse can carry on its back less than a quarter of the weight it can draw in a cart. Also, on the unfenced crofts, it would need to be tethered; and its wintering would keep a paying stirk, whereas a horse (unless hired, or a mare breeding foals) brings in no direct profit in money. In a similar place in Ireland, donkeys would be used: their keep is negligible, and they can do an amazing amount of work for their size. But they, like pigs, have never appealed to the Scottish crofters, and the only one on the estate was introduced by a stranger.

I was lucky in not having to buy saddlery. The Indian cavalry saddle, that had carried me on my ride from Cornwall, fitted Blossom fairly well, as did the Army pack-saddle that accompanied me on the same journey. I had leather-bound canvas wallets for polite goods, and a pair of hazel creels in which peats, seaweed, sacks of coal, and cans of paraffin, boxes of stores, and bags of cattle feed could easily be stowed. For dung, I used the boxes described in the previous chapter. Hay and corn were carried in roped bundles slung from the hooks of the pack-saddle.

For one who has not the knack of carrying burdens, or any liking for it, any kind of horse is better than none; but I must admit that a pack-saddle is a very poor substitute for a cart. Not only does it carry so much less, but it requires far more patience and management, especially on rough ground, and, for real comfort, needs two people to each horse. The load must balance exactly and, in theory (though this was rarely possible in a one-man show like mine), should be loaded and unloaded from both sides at once. To lift anything really heavy onto a horse's back is a strain for one person, especially as the saddle will slip to the side you have loaded first. I always tried to divide the load into small lots – four or even six units – instead of two; but this often meant opening hundredweight bags and emptying half the contents into another, and our supply of sound bags was lamentably small.

Then there were loads like timber, firewood, and packages

of odd shape that would not go into creels but must be roped to the saddle direct. The roping needed to be very tight, or things would soon come adrift. Sometimes an ill-balanced load needed a stone added to the lighter side, and nearly always girths must be tightened on the way. Blossom was very patient. If a load began to slip on the road, there was no fuss or capering; she merely stopped dead and when I looked round (for I always led her on a long rope, leaving her to follow and pick her own way) would give me a withering glance of contempt. Even if the slip were complete, with saddle and load dangling under her belly, she did no more than assume a sulky, martyred expression. Such accidents were better avoided, for one rarely met anyone on the Smirisary path and it was hard to clear and repack a capsized load alone.

I soon found that the hazel creels were not strong enough for some of the work they had to do; they soon lost their shape, and constantly needed repair or replacement. I had long been racking my brains for a substitute, when I happened to see a pair of those iron panniers used by the Forestry Commission to carry fencing stobs on the hill. A modified version of these might suit; and hearing that the Invermoriston blacksmith made them, I ordered a pair for myself and they have proved most serviceable.

At first I imagined my neighbours would be glad to make use of Blossom. But nervousness, inexperience, sheer conservatism, and the fear of being blamed for some accident made most of them hang back; only Angus Ruairidh, who had worked with ponies in a deer forest, ventured to take her out alone. To most of them, accustomed from boyhood to the carrying of burdens, a pony was only an embarrassment; indeed, I would often carry a load myself sooner than trouble to catch and saddle the mare. The pack-saddle, with its iron arches and hooks, was very heavy, and the hauling of it from the stable, the lifting into position, and the tightening of muddy girths and recalcitrant straps was a job I disliked more than any other.

When I first came to Smirisary, there were no fences anywhere and the occasional low stone dykes, with gaps closed by a stick or a loose iron bar, were no obstacle to a roving pony. Tethering was the only solution. I bought a length of chain and ropes complete with snap-hook, swivel, and an iron pin, which could be driven into the ground where required. I wondered how Blossom would take to the tether and had visions of her galloping wildly in circles, winding the chain round stones and tussocks, until she herself was involved in a python-like embrace. I need not have bothered. She managed the tether like a lady. Her legs were never entangled and if by chance the chain did get foul of something, she would stand in quiet resignation until someone passed near, when she would nicker earnestly for release. Occasionally her stance did not please her at all, and she would refuse to graze, walking restlessly about and tossing her head. She never cared to be left in a remote corner out of sight of people and houses. Having no company of her own species, she was dependent on man's companionship and liked to be near us when we worked. A tethered horse is handy, but makes a good deal of work. The pitch must be changed often – at least twice a day in summer and four times in winter, and there must be shelter from the prevailing wind. Not caring to leave her tethered and unattended at night, I used to stable her in the byre. In the depths of winter, when to take her in at sundown would make too long a night inside, I used to leave her out till my own bed-time. Then, torch in hand, I wound in the long, cold length of chain, pulled up the pin, and led her home.

Actually the pin was a later addition. At first I moored Blossom like a boat to a stone, or tied her to some convenient bush. Sometimes the knot would slip or the branch break, and my lady would wander off, usually to someone else's ground, or, climbing the brae behind my house, join Dolly at Allt Ruadh. The chink of the chain trailing over the stones might attract my attention, or Annie, spying her, would whistle. These excursions, apart from the time they wasted, caused little trouble, as she never left the path or took to the hill, and her whiteness made her easy to spot. Sometimes indeed, she was the excuse for the walk I always enjoyed but rarely found time to take.

I specially remember one evening at the end of September 1944. It had been a fine summer and the crops were all in so that we could enjoy, much earlier than usual, the soothing and spacious peace of autumn. Sitting at supper in the window, I could see no clouds in the sky, except, low down, faint pencillings of cirrus, too thin to veil the golden ball of the sun which rolled slowly over the horizon, round as an orange and no less unattainable. On the topmost branch of the elder, a robin raised his sweet, frail song against the immensity of sea and imminent night. By the shore, curlews were crying – a sign of rain according to Angus, but if this were true, it would need to rain more often even than it does. As the shadows fell and colour ebbed from the world, the lights flashed out from Eigg and the lonely rock of Bo Fhaskadail in Ardnamurchan.

By this time it was dark indoors, and I was just lighting my new Tilley lamp when the whistle shrilled from Tigh Ruairidh. These blasts usually meant that Blossom had slipped her tether; and so it was. In the quiet verge of night, I heard a voice calling in Gaelic, "The horse is away up the pass!" Having started to light the Tilley, I must needs finish, or waste precious methylated spirit; so the pony had a long start. But on a night like this, with neither wind nor midges to annoy her, I knew that she would not get far, and took my time. Climbing the stony path that leads over the Bealach to Samalaman and Glenuig, I found Blossom just on the further side, where the track drops by rocky ledges and pockets of bog to the peaty flats of the Laran Beag. There was another pony on that ground, with whom she fought and played in turns, both being mares. But this time they had not found one another and Blossom was grazing alone; and upon her flanks lay the ghostly sheen with which night transfigures the daylight dullness of a pale beast. I caught her with a bit of bread and led her homeward, halting as always at the top of the pass to look about me. This place, surrounded by low stone dykes now falling into ruin, was called Faing Mhic Phail, or MacPhail's fold – one of the many old cattle enclosures that are scattered over the hill ground of Smirisary. Whoever herded up there was in truth on the roof of our little world, for he could see the sprawling length of Ardnamurchan, the Small Isles, the hills of Skye, and in very clear weather, like a humped cloud on the horizon, the distant peak of Heaval in Barra.

As I stood there, leaning upon the pony's shoulder, my eyes rested on the spiry peaks of the Cuillin, which for the last twenty years have never been far out of sight or long out of mind. In the clearness of the north wind, every pinnacle was sharply defined, yet the whole range seemed floating, detached in space, remote as the clouds that drifted above it. The robin's song had ceased, leaving a silence filled only with the vast sighing of the deep. Always, when coming to Smirisary or leaving it, I stop at Faing Mhic Phail to look and listen. Coming, the sea noise welcomes me home, though house and croft lie still unseen at the foot of the brae. And when I leave, I must look intently on everything and listen to every sound, lest I should never return. Every parting is possibly final, though for those without second sight the last hour has nothing to distinguish it from any other.

When I acquired the pin, it was but seldom that Blossom escaped, though, had she known her strength, one jerk of her sturdy neck would have broken the rope. On calm, sunny days, she would often lie stretched full length and allow Augusta, the young Ayrshire heifer, to lick her all over. In windy weather she would walk restlessly about, demanding frequent shifts, and whinnying to passers-by. If thunder came, she would bolt. During the war, when we often heard heavy firing, it was sometimes hard to distin-

guish God's artillery from man's. But Blossom always knew.
At firing, however loud, she only flinched, but thunder
made her panic and at the first warning of an approaching
storm I would shut her in the stable till it was over.

One wild October afternoon I was too late. A veil of
blackness swept up from the west and, in the thunder
squall that followed, I saw through a white mist of hail the
terrified pony galloping over the croft land. There was a
blinding flash and when I looked again she was gone. A
few minutes later, when the squall had passed, I went in
pursuit, following her tracks in the soft ground. Caught in
a bush behind Tigh Lachain I found the tether, complete
with pin and headstall which she had pulled over her head
without breaking. Blossom herself was quietly grazing near
the Samalaman march fence. I led her home, and found
Smirisary full of a *beithir* or thunderbolt, which a herdsman had seen falling in the Laran Mor. A ball of fire, he
said, had fallen, scattering the cattle: and later we found,
near the place indicated, a scar on a rock and a trench
scored in the ground.

But thunderbolts were less alarming than drifting mines.
One of these, on a quiet Sunday afternoon in 1942, ex-
ploded in the little bay behind Tigh Ruairidh. Fortunately
a substantial knollie protected the house, which suffered
no damage but the breaking of the little back window.
Fragments of stone were scattered all over the croft, and
Angus, who was on the byre path at the time, assured me
that the blast lifted him off his feet. Later, when the war
was over, a stranded mine was seen just south of Achadh an
Aonaich, and reported to Father Bradley, who telephoned
to the authorities. A disposal squad arrived and we were
told to keep ourselves and our cattle indoors. Anxiously
we awaited the Big Bang. It never came.

Far more intriguing was a blackish object which Sandy
spotted at about seven o'clock on a summer's evening,
floating some fifty yards from the shore. He pointed it out
to me. It was not unlike a seal's head, but no seal was ever

so long on the surface and we agreed that it was probably
a mine. There was a fresh wind blowing from the south
but the object, whatever it was, remained stationary. We
concluded that the mooring chain of the mine – if mine
it were – must have fouled a rock as it trailed along the
bottom. This caused us some anxious thought. Had the
mine been free, and the wind still from the south, it would
soon have drifted past Smirisary and away towards the uninhabited shores of Rhu Arisaig; but if it remained where
it was till the wind veered west, it might easily break loose
and come ashore at Port nam Feannagan or the Lon Liath – far too near to be pleasant. We watched it until long
after sunset; and the sinister black ball remained as it was.
Then at last, when we were resigning ourselves to an uneasy night, we saw that the thing was moving and ever getting smaller, as it drifted away to the north. The wind held,
and we breathed again!

To return for a moment to Blossom. In June 1945, I was
to spend a short holiday at Fernaig and it occurred to me
that I might take her with me, travelling across the hills to
Glenshiel, where I would pick up the Cluanie – Kyle road,
and then return through Skye, and by steamer from Ar-
madale to Mallaig. The route promised to be interesting,
lying across country unknown to me and in any case unfre-
quented. From Loch Ailort I went by Meobal to the head
of Loch Morar and thence through Glen Pean to Loch
Arkaig. From there I crossed a high pass into Glen Kingie
and on to Loch Quoich. June is usually the driest month
of the year in the Highlands but that June was appallingly
wet; it rained most of the time and every river and burn
was in spate. Loch Quoich, with its mean annual rainfall
of over one hundred inches, is anyway, one of the wettest
places in Britain – too wet, I was told, for hay to be made or
peats dried. I had intended to take a hill track from Loch
Quoich into Glenshiel but the keeper, at whose house I
spent the night, warned me that the burns were too big
for safety and I proceeded drearily by road, in two days

of incessant wind and rain, by Tomdown and Cluanie to Dornie and thence to Stromeferry, where they were astonished to see me arrive in such weather. This ride brought home to me, as nothing else could have done, the extreme desolation and depopulation of these inland glens. Most of the houses marked on the ordnance map were empty and ruinous; the grass in some places was knee deep, with never a beast in sight, and you might travel all day and meet no living soul.

Blossom seemed awed by these vast and frowning solitudes. Often the track was hard to find, sometimes it vanished altogether, and the map, saturated by the everlasting downpour, dropped to pieces and was abandoned long before I reached Loch Quoich. There were bogs and narrow paths with awkward drops, and more than once a flooded river to ford, because the bridge marked on the map proved to be a suspension footbridge impossible for a horse. When, at our midday halts, I turned her loose to graze, she always kept near me, as if dependent on my company. And once in Glen Pean, when I was uncertain of the way and left her tethered while I climbed a rock to prospect, she never took her eyes off me till I returned, greeting me then with a whinny of pleasure and relief.

11

Lovely May

EVERY season, even the dead of winter, had its own grace; yet all the year I found myself counting the days till May. The lingering evenings, the short twilit nights, the song of birds, the flowers, the fresh brilliance of things still young but no more frail and menaced as in April: how lovely it all could be, provided that there was enough rain and the spring work were finished or nearly so. The merry month was apt to be full of hard work, for the long fine evenings tempted me to stay out till dark, trying to overtake a score of urgent and competing jobs. There was much to do in the garden and everything to do at the peats, and I never knew which to put first. We in the Highlands are often blamed for rising late, but we also work late; and it is not good to burn the candle at both ends till the two flames meet and destroy us.

Of the four Mays I have so far seen in Smirisary, two were wet and one exceptionally dry. A wet May pleases the farmer and gardener, for everything shoots ahead and the grass comes when it is most needed. And for sheer delight of the eye, there is nothing to equal those broken showery days, with their exquisite rainbows, and the new-washed sheen of the earth when the sun comes out at the tail of a shower: though if you are late with your corn, or working a bare fallow, or trying to get a fine tilth for grass-seeds, those frequent showers can be a curse.

I always loved my westward-facing house, not only for the glow of afternoon sunshine, but because I could watch the clearing after a storm. A Highland home should never face south or south-east, for from this quarter comes most of the dirty weather, the gales and driving rain. I shall always remember a wet day in May, when I was sitting at dinner, cursing because I could not get out to the croft. The south wind was beating on the gable, rumbling in the chimney. Sheets of rain drove slantingly down the glen and waves, short and snarling, raced past the Seann Rudha, gathering force as they passed beyond the shelter of the land. The islands were lost in vapour, and the Minch, with its now unbroken horizon, might have been the open Atlantic. Then I noticed that the run of the waves had changed; there was a slight inshore set, raindrops pattered on the window instead of racing past it, and gusts came puffing under the door. Low down on the murky horizon came a suggestion of light; and to eyes familiar with their outlines, the islands began to take shape once more, misty at first, then more distinct until behind them appeared a band of clear sky, faintly coloured, with a veil of rain falling over it, which blurred the verge of luminous clouds beyond. Then the sun came out afar and shone on the white houses of Eigg and the lovely symmetrical curves of Muck, though clouds still hung on the peaks of Rhum and the Cuillin were invisible. As the edge of the raincloud passed with a freshening west wind, the sea came to life in a thousand sparkles, under a sky of rain-washed speedwell blue. The clouds began to rise on Rhum, revealing slopes of shadow and sunshine. On the horizon, and partly below it, was piled a line of brilliant cumulus clouds smudged here and there with passing showers. The water brimmed in the burn and every flower and blade of grass was glittering with raindrops.

The grass-land in Smirisary abounded with bluebells and kingcups in sharply defined zones, bluebells on the drier red soil, and kingcups on the black peat. Even on the smallest plots, these strips of yellow and blue lay side by side, giving an exquisite enamelled appearance which delighted the eye, though, from the agricultural point of view, bluebells and kingcups are unpalatable and undesirable weeds.

Early in May, the arable ground of the township was closed to stock. We were all busy repairing drystone dykes and stopping gaps with sticks and bushes. Cattle were driven to the hill, in the hope (too often vain) that they would stay there till the evening milking. Herding, which in winter might be no more than a traditional way of passing time, now became a serious if not a heart-breaking affair. All beasts were housed at night, which at least saved us from worrying about midnight raids. Though there was new grass springing in the open grazings of the Port and the Faing Mor, the cows knew well enough that there was better in the forbidden ground of the Goirtean and the Blaran Boidheach and were for ever trying to force their way into those sacred enclosures.

Worse than the cattle were the sheep; they were harder to fence against and were free to roam where they pleased by night. The last job of a long day's work was a sheep patrol, when Angus or myself or both of us would go out at the darkening; and if any sheep were in sight, we chased them away beyond Achadh an Aonaich, in the hope that they would not return before morning. There was also a dawn patrol, which fell on me, because my window commanded the slopes down which the sheep would invade the crofts. I tried to wake at five, and if any marauders were visible, I would open the door, let out Dileas after them and then return to bed. Once I was roused by the rumble of falling stones, and found that three of the brutes had climbed the garden wall and were peacefully grazing on the tiny lawn in the middle.

In 1946, the sheep were particularly troublesome. The spring was late and cold, with a severe drought in May. The grass never got a proper start and the hill was as bare as a board. Ewes with young lambs to nourish were mad for a bite of green and it was almost impossible to keep them off the crofts. Angus had lost his beautiful collie, Dane, who had picked up a poisoned bait for foxes, and was left with only a half-trained pup and the keen but inefficient Dileas. When the sheep broke in for the third morning in succession, he remarked gloomily that if this continued we should have

no hay at all. But as every farmer and crofter says the same
thing every year, and there is always plenty, I did not take his
pessimism very seriously.

Exquisite as it is, there is a treachery in May which no
one appreciates until he comes to deal intimately with
the land. In 1945 and 1946 came a visitation of late frosts
which ruined the fruit crop in many parts of Scotland. Being so near the sea, we suffered less; but in 1945 I lost half
the black-currants and some of the strawberries. In 1946
we had six weeks of cold, drying winds which checked the
growth of all things. Most of my earlier garden sowings
came to nothing and only the extreme moistness of the
situation prevented the grass-seeds, sown in the middle of
May, from being a complete failure. The hay was done and
the wretched cows, one in full milk and the other heavy
in calf, could find but little outside. It was difficult even to
provide them with water, for the small burns and pools on
the hill were dry. Mercifully our well held out, and there
was a trickle in the main Smirisary burn; but these, being
surrounded by arable ground now closed for hay, were not
available for beasts. I dug out and cleaned Tobar Mairea-
read, the old well on the shore, and it made a useful water hole. Lovely as the sunshine was, one's enjoyment was
lessened by the perpetual struggle with drought and by
the brittleness of nerves that comes with a prolonged spell
of dry weather. I can still remember the nervous tension
caused by the great summer droughts of 1911 and 1921,
when we stared at the brassy dome of the sky, watching for
a change that never came. It is amazing how three or four
rainless weeks in spring or early summer can dry up a land
so wet as the West Highlands. It is not that the autumn
and winter rains are actually excessive, but that the rate of
evaporation at this season is very slow so that a day's rain
will leave a sea of mud that lasts a week. In May or June, all
trace would be gone in a night.

May 1946 was spoilt for me by too much work, so that I
felt like one who runs after a bus he has no hope of overtak-

ing. For some time I had been dreading the departure of my excellent neighbours, the Gillies family. I suspected that, as soon as Katie's husband was clear of the army, the young people would leave the Goirtean and take their father with them. For some time Sandy had been finding the work of the croft very heavy; there was no younger man to help him with the peats and the manuring or with the carrying of coal demanded by a newer economy. The burden was as much moral as physical, for a burden shared is more than halved, and to work always alone produces (except in certain rare natures) a feeling of despondency, even of abandonment. He had begun to hate the racket of storms on his iron roof, and after one exceptionally violent gale, during which he had not taken off his clothes, I heard him say that he would rather be a tramp on the road than endure many more nights like that. The Goirtean was the home of his fathers, where he had lived and worked all his married life; but it held sorrowful associations, for it was there that he lost his wife when the five children were all under nine, and later, when he had reared them himself unaided, he lost first a daughter and then both sons in the war. The death of Simon, the younger one, far away in Burma was a blow which it took all the old man's faith and courage to meet; and I do not think he ever cared much for the Goirtean afterwards. Yet, when he worked away at the reclamation of his new potato ground and laid a thatch of rushes on the noisy iron roof of his house, I began to hope that after all he might be intending to stay.

But Jimmy MacLean, his son-in-law, was offered the post of estate carpenter with a house between Samalaman and Glenuig and in the spring of 1946, when the stirks were ready to go to the Salen sale, the family packed up and went. The flitting was done piecemeal, something or other being removed each time anyone went to Glenuig; and, as time passed, the house, stripped of all that gave it character and comfort, began to look like a place where one camps for the night. The last things were taken away in Sandy's boat which, at the top of the spring tides, came into the narrow landing-place at the Lon Liath. Strings of neighbours ran to and fro, carrying in creels or ropes the last of the household possessions. Finally the hens and the cattle departed and the old house, blind and fireless, was left to its ghosts. No one living could remember a day when smoke had not risen from its chimney.

As my own land was inextricably mixed up with Sandy's, it seemed a sensible thing to take the whole croft and put a fence round it. A larger holding with more cows would justify me in getting the help I so badly needed. I planned either to let Sandy's house to a family who would give me a little assistance, or to use it as a bothy for a single man or woman. So on May 28th, I became the official occupier of the Goirtean. Two members of the Land Court, one being the Gaelic-speaking representative, the delightful Colin MacDonald, came with Graham to value the buildings and improvements. We all went round and looked at everything, chattering amicably in Gaelic, and Colin was tickled by the anxiety of Sandy and myself that the other one should have fair play. The imposing dunghill was measured and valued at £7.

It took me some time and trouble to find a tenant for the house and, in the meantime, I had far too much to do. Luckily for me most of the work I do is enjoyable, so that I find it difficult to say where work ends and play begins. Hence I do not bother about hours or days, provided that I can avoid rushing and over-fatigue. It is wonderful how much a person can do by quietly pottering, day in, day out. But the knowledge that there are at least six jobs waiting to be done, of which you must choose the most urgent and leave the rest for sheer want of time or strength, takes the heart out of the worker; and so it was then. When a man goes into a farm at the May term, the spring work is done by the outgoing tenant and is paid for at the valuation. But on a croft, it seems, the incomer does it himself. Luckily, Sandy had taken a creel of dung to the Lon Liath every day from

December onwards and had thus accumulated a good supply on the ground itself, which was most useful for my own potatoes and kale. But I had all the grass-land to manure, as well as about an acre of digging.

Sandy's arable plot was the cause of much labour. It was fenced, but not against rabbits, and I had to procure and erect netting in a great hurry. The kale was sown in the garden and transplanted later; a third of the seedlings were promptly eaten by an enterprising rabbit, which tunnelled under some inches of sunk netting. Luckily, I had replacements and the raid was not repeated. The potatoes, with the help of Angus, were planted at the end of April; but everything else was late and all the time I was chasing the clock, like a busy housewife who has overslept herself, or the objectors to the reformed calendar, who went about shouting, "Give us back our eleven days!" The carrots – there were thirty rows of them – were sown too thick, for I forgot to mix the seed with earth or sand. They came up excellently but the thinning of them was a back-breaking and tedious job.

The cabbages, savoys, etc. had to be planted twice owing to the severe drought. Then, in June, when the weather broke up finally and completely and the grass verges became lush and damp, armies of slugs emerged and mowed down the young carrots four or five feet inwards from the edges. They destroyed the cabbages by swarming up the stalks and devouring the leaves. Weeds, especially creeping buttercup and persicaria, began to flourish inordinately. The ground was badly in need of lime and, although I had plenty stored in the Samalaman boathouse, there had been no opportunity of bringing it to the Goirtean.

The subsequent history of the arable plot was mingled success and disaster. The carrots were excellent and we lived all the summer on the delicate thinnings. The potatoes proved a fair crop but became very dirty. The kale was surprisingly good, and so was the corn in spite of the ridiculous lateness of its sowing. Cabbage and curly kale promised well, until one day in September, came sudden doom – how and when, I shall never know, for the ground was in the far corner of Sandy's croft and invisible from either house. I went down to pull carrots and was confronted with an appalling desolation. The strong fence was broken inwards; the corn, then nearly fit for cutting, was a mat of fouled and trampled straw, with all the grain destroyed; half the kale, nearly all the cabbages, as well as the potato shaws, were eaten to the ground. The carrots alone remained unscathed. This was the work of cattle – thank God, not mine, nor those of any neighbour in Smirisary. The fence was broken outwards in another place, showing that the beasts had been discovered and driven out again. I was never nearer to tears, even when the first fruits of my young apple trees were stripped unripe by a child and thrown away, with a nibble in each.

Later, there was an amusing incident, which gave me much scope for chaffing my neighbours. There were no deer on the Glenuig estate but from time to time they came in from neighbouring forests and raided gardens and potato pits. In 1942, when I first tried to grow thousand-headed kale for a winter-calving cow, the whole lot disappeared in one night. Since then no deer had visited Smirisary and I was just wondering if I need bother to raise the fence to six feet, when Angus reported that he and another man had seen a stag on the hill. He lent me some rolls of sheep netting, the seven-foot poles I had cut for hay tripods were used as temporary standards, and we worked feverishly to make the plot safe. When it was all done and we were sitting back with relief, the stag proved to have been a half-wild billy-goat strayed from Glenfinnan!

The long dry spell suited the peats and all my neighbours, untroubled with gardens or green crops, secured theirs early and easily. I had long since abandoned the Laran Mor and opened a small bank at Faing Mhic Phail, from which the peat could easily be carried home with the pony. On this high shelf above the sea, open and free from midges, it was a pleasure to work. But I could only snatch an hour or two at odd times and, when there is no helper to spread, the cutter must stop every few minutes to dispose of the pile of sods beside him. As luck would have it, I needed more this year as the new tenants at the Goirtean, arriving in July, were too late to get much for themselves. I shared my small supply, which by December was finished.

How much I longed, in these busy days, that I could be multiplied by two or even three, for there is nothing more annoying than to see everything at a standstill in the place where one is not. One of the biggest jobs was the fencing of the Goirtean hay-ground: but of this more in the sequel.

There were many compensations, of which the memory abides when the annoyances they balanced are forgotten. Not only the solid satisfaction of the sure, if jolting and fragmentary, achievement but the beauty of the visible world and the inward peace that came with it. I was never too tired to gather the cows from the hill at the darkening and watch the last light fall on their white rumps as they slithered down the steep byre path, their sweet milky breath mingling with the perfumes of the wild. Or to pause after the last load of dung and, leaning on the pony's neck, watch the sunset fading behind the Cuillin and hear the moaning of the surf and, far away, in the willow scrub of the Lon Liath, the last song of a blackbird.

12

Cows

By the end of September 1943, I had my first season's hay secure in the barn and could think about buying a cow. The land I worked at that time would not winter more than one beast in addition to the pony, so I resolved to get an autumn calver, which would provide us all with milk through the winter. I knew that with wartime livestock rations and no home-grown turnips or grain I could not hope for a big flow; but if I rid myself of the calf as quickly as possible there would be milk for everyone, and butter for a few, until the crofters' cattle calved in spring.

Autumn-calving cows are always dear and difficult to procure, especially in the Highlands. There was nothing to be had locally, nor was it easy for me to get away to a sale. So I asked the salesman who had sent me Blossom to keep a look-out for a suitable beast.

It is one thing to send a cow by train to Lochailort and quite another to get her home to Smirisary. The Laird once said that, in a place like ours, all cattle should be bred on the spot and kept there for life; nor was he far wrong. Since that time, the store-boat has occasionally transported cows, even a bull; but for so risky an operation, the weather and tide must be just right and the beast a quiet one. For a cow heavy in calf, the crumbling slippery piers were altogether too risky. We had no choice but to walk. If the cow were very quiet and you met no other cattle on the road, one person could lead her on a rope as one might a horse. But you were much safer and quicker with a companion, especially if you were a mere woman. Unfortunately, everyone was busy lifting potatoes and none of the men could spare a whole day, so Maisie Bright volunteered to come with me. She never did a kinder service.

The goods train was expected at Lochailort about one o'clock so we had plenty of time to go up on the store-boat and lunch at the hotel before it arrived. The day was dry when we left home but by the time we reached Lochailort rain was driving before a rising southerly wind. The train came in and the cow was led from the track – a brown and white polled beast, sleek and gentle, and obviously near her time. We were prepared to be a long while on the road, but not for the pace at which the poor brute started. I was at her head, with the halter in my hands, while Maisie, who should merely have prodded behind, held another rope as a safety anchor, and well that she did. The cow set off at a run, luckily down the right road, towing us helpless behind. As we crossed the bridge, she nearly threw me into the river. On she rushed, past Inverailort Castle and up the steep, stony ascent of the Bealach Breac; where the wind and rain lashed us without mercy.

The Bealach, though apparently sheltered from the south by the peaks of Roshven and An Stac which rose direct from the loch side, was in fact most horribly exposed to a downdraught from the funnel shaped corrie which divided them, especially at the summit where you looked down upon Alisary. By the time we reached this point, the cow's strength was beginning to flag and her pace slackened. The wind, hauling ahead in an awful squall, shrieked down the corrie and literally brought her to a standstill while, gasping for breath, we cowered in the shelter of her capacious body. Long before we reached Roshven, the poor beast was tired out and the problem was no longer how to keep up with her, but how to get her home at all. By rights we should have made a break at Roshven farm, with hay for the cow and tea for ourselves. But we both knew that if once we stopped, even to empty the water from our shoes, we should never get going again. So we plodded on, more and more slowly, I towing and Maisie prodding, with many a song to cheer the cow and ourselves. When we reached Glenuig, the brief daylight was almost gone, and Maisie suggested that I should put the cow in her byre and spend the night with herself at the Cottage. This was done. Obviously we could never get to Smirisary that night, perhaps not even to Samalaman. The byre was on a brae above the house, approached by one of those steep muddy paths in which Glenuig abounded. When we had settled the cow with hay and bedding, it was quite dark, and we dripped our way into an inky house with no matches handy. Thank God there was a fire, which the thoughtful priest had lighted against our return, but as yet no hot water for baths. We had to change to the skin and it was not easy to find enough clothes, whether of the male or female sort.

Next morning we took the cow, which I called Maisie, to Smirisary, and two days later she calved. The calf – a bull – was sold locally at three weeks old, and there was milk for everyone in the township. Maisie was delightfully quiet – "*martan gun dragh*",* as Sandy put it. She ran with the Gillies' cows all day and all I had to do was to drive her across to the Goirtean in the morning and let her into my own byre at night. Nor did she resent sharing her lodging with the pony, who occupied the other stall.

One difficulty, especially in summer, was that I had no dairy, neither had any of the crofters. Most of them kept the milk in a closet, or even in a cupboard in the "room" or parlour, where there was rarely a fire. Mine was in the kitchen, where I neither lived nor slept nor ran a fire, as my simple meals were cooked on an oil-stove. In the corner furthest from the stove was a table covered with a white cloth, on which were set the skimming basins, the strainer, cream jar, skimmer, milk jugs, and plates of butter. At first I had no tinned skimmer, but used, in local fashion, a clam shell pierced with holes. This primitive but effective utensil was very pretty, with a charming transparency when held against the light. I was careful with my washing and scalding, and never found that either milk or butter suffered from the lack of a special dairy, good as it would have been to possess one.

* A little cow without bother.

My butter was considered the best in the place. Long ago, at Achnadarroch, I had made it; but then we had the milk of several cows, and it was worth while to have a butter worker and an end-over-end churn. But at Smirisary there was only one cow; and the milk of one cow, when you are supplying several households and using a little cream as well, does not go very far. The small glass table churns were then unobtainable and I depended on Annie for the use of her wooden hexagonal box churn, which had taken the place of the old fashioned tall kind with a plunger. Annie's churn was rather like a large musical box; it had clappers within and a handle at one side, and a bung which didn't work, so that you had to pour away the buttermilk and washing waters from the top. You had also to hold the lid with one hand while you turned the handle with the other. If he were not too busy, Angus would take a spell at the handle, and there was much talk and laughter, and tea to finish up with. We had some trouble to get the temperature right as no one had a thermometer. Sometimes Annie would sprinkle the churn with holy water from a bottle. I worked and made up the butter with Scotch hands, printing the pats with various kinds of chevron patterns which were much admired. Everyone wanted the butter, though only a few could get it: one pat went to Dorothy Stokes in England, and another was exchanged with Maisie for eggs.

All this winter milk and butter sounds very fine, but, as usual, there was a snag. Autumn and winter calving is unnatural, and though you may induce a cow, and even more easily a heifer, to oblige you once, you will not find it so easy to continue to do so. There is always a strong tendency to revert to the natural spring season. An October calver should take the bull in January, if she is to calve again at the same time; but too often, especially if feeding-stuffs are scarce, there will be no heat till June or July and thus no calf till March or April following. The wretched Maisie did not come in heat till September, nearly a year after calving. This was hopeless; I had to sell her, needless to say for a song. In February, when all the crofters' cows were dry, I went to Oban sale with Graham and bought Brigid, whom I have still.

Brigid was a cross Ayrshire, very nearly all white, with a few dark brown spots on face, muzzle, and ears. She had the trim shape, neat silky udder, and symmetrical horns of the breed. She was newly calved, and I had to arrange for her to be milked at Fort William, where a nephew of the MacNeils, who was devoted to cows, happened to be a signalman. By the time she arrived – this time without incident – everyone was without milk and thankful to see her.

The snag about Brigid – otherwise a most excellent beast – was that she gave no visible signs of heat, so that the first few times were missed, and she was late in calving. The second year she did not calve till the first week in April, and the third year not till the end of May, thus dashing all hopes of keeping her as a winter cow. August came, and still no sign of heat, and I was forced to let her run with the bull at Samalaman, though she was still in full milk, and we were very busy with the hay. It seemed easier to milk Brigid at Samalaman and bring down the pail, than to drive the cow up and down each day; so Myfanwy, my student assistant, and myself went up in turn, morning and evening, milked the cow and brought down the heavy pail of milk. This went on for sixteen days, until at last, Alec Gillies came rushing down to tell us that she was served. But so great was Alec's reputation for romancing that no one believed him, especially as another white cow had been to the bull on the same day. But his story was confirmed by other older and more reliable witnesses, and with great joy we took her home.

When in the spring of 1946, I acquired the Goirtean, I had enough land to winter two more beasts. Sandy was taking with him his two younger cows but there was old Daisy, a cross Shorthorn with crooked horns, who had been the boss cow of the Goirtean herd for many years. She was a good milker, very quiet, and knew every hole and corner of the hill. Strictly speaking, Daisy was too old to be worth buying: but between the price I got for her when dry at the end of the season, the price of her excellent calf, and the value of all the milk and butter she gave me, I certainly did not lose by the transaction. She soon learned to come home to my byre, where she had Blossom's stall. The pony was housed in a small building at the Goirtean and Sandy's byre was used as a store for peats and bracken.

A little later, Graham sold me a pure-bred Ayrshire yearling heifer. She was very quiet, not to say stolid in disposition, but had never been led on a rope; and when Myfanwy and I light-heartedly proposed going to fetch her from Samalaman, Angus shook his head and insisted on bringing her down himself. It was just as well. We met him at Faing Mhic Phail, hot and exhausted, with the lovely little creature plunging and straining, and making circles round him, head down and tail in air. Luckily the new fence at the Port was completed for Augusta, as we called her, pined for her old companions and was always trying to get back to Samalaman. She even managed to slither down the sheer face of the crags above Port nam Feannagan and wandered about in the uncut hay below, watched curiously by Brigid and Daisy, who longed to follow but did not dare.

In the matter of calves I had been unlucky. I wanted a heifer to rear; but all the calves I ever had at Smirisary were males and, owing to the shortage of linseed cake and other feed, I was not anxious to winter them. This rather shocked the neighbours, whose main source of income was the sale of stirks at the annual spring sale at Salen, Loch Sunart. My object was not so much the making of money, which loses its charm when one can buy so little with it, as the production of human food, and especially of butter whose price is above rubies. And so I was not keen on using some 150 gallons of milk on rearing a stirk. With the yearling, on the other hand, I had the first difficult winter behind me; the second was only a matter of hay.

In one thing I was very fortunate: I had no herding. All my neighbours, except Sandy whose pasture had fewer real or imaginary dangers, spent several hours a day sitting with cows on the hill or working in places where they could keep watch over their elusive charges. Cattle – grazing, straying, or marauding – were at the back of everyone's mind; in summer, lest they broke into the arable, your own or another's; in winter, lest they fell down a cliff or into a drain. Cattle are valuable and represent a crofter's capital; but it is impossible, even were it desirable, to eliminate all risk. If there were less herding and more work, the extra gain would more than offset the very occasional loss of a beast. Daily herding is a thing to which you must be born; if you are, no doubt its absence would leave a void which nothing else could fill. For my own part, herding drives me mad for I hate standing about. When we are at work, let us work; and when we play, let it be with a free mind.

As long as Sandy was at the Goirtean, my cow went with his; after he left, I had the arable fenced. On my part of the hill there were no drains and but few rock-faces, and the cattle had to take their chance. By agreement with the only other crofter who shared any part of this grazing, I fenced the Port and the Faing Mor and thus was able to keep the cows out at night in the summer and qualify for the subsidy.

When Daisy was sold at Christmas 1946, I had only Brigid now nearly dry and not due again until the end of May. The thought of four months without milk or butter for anyone appalled me. I was spending the Christmas holiday at Fernaig, and arranged to go on from there and meet Graham at a sale in Oban on January 8th, where I would try to get another winter calver. I had saved feeding stuffs, including the whole of Blossom's work-horse ration, and part of the kale, and the whole of the carrots had survived the disaster of the previous September. There was plenty of hay in the barn and I could afford to do the cow well, if I could get her.

But this expedition seemed doomed to failure from the first. I left Fernaig in an easterly gale, with the threat of snow on the blurred horizon. The harbour-master at Kyle thought that the Mallaig steamer would not call, but she did, though it was all she could do to get clear of the pier in the teeth of that blast. I have never seen an off-shore wind raise such a sea. In the narrows of Kyle Rhea, where the ebb was setting strongly down channel, there was a white welter of waves breaking in all directions as at the centre of a cyclone. By the time we reached Mallaig, a few flakes were beginning to fall. At Fort William, I caught a bus to North Ballachulish with but little hope that the ferry would be running. The wind was howling round the bus and one glance at the white water in the strait was enough. No ferry that day, nor for several days after, and there was nothing for it but to sit in the bus and go up the loch to Kinlochleven, down the other side to Ballachulish, and through Glencoe to Tyndrum, whence one could get to Oban by train. It was now snowing in earnest and the rest of that miserable bus ride was a slow laborious fight against a blizzard which plastered the windscreen with a thick layer of white. Darkness had fallen, and even in day-light it would have been too thick to see the famous glen. We stopped once or twice, and I didn't like it. I was sick-ening for 'flu, and had no wish to spend the night snowed up in Glencoe.

At Tyndrum, there were two railway stations, a lot of pine trees laden with snow, and a warm, brightly-lit, com-fortable hotel. I let the Oban train go and sank into a warm comfortable bed. The plucky little bus started back on the long trail to Fort William. I thought of it often during the night with a kind of affection. It was so good not to be in it.

At Oban there was no snow, but it was still blowing hard; and when, about two hours before the sale, I went into the market byre to inspect the entries, there were only about half-a-dozen beasts there. Mainland roads were blocked with snow and cattle from the islands were waiting for steamers that never called. A wire came in from Graham to say that he and his shepherd were stuck at Lochaline: the Mull boat had passed without calling. This was a blow. Their company and help would have cheered me. I was feeling ill and horribly cold, and most disinclined to take part in a sale where I knew no one.

When the sale began there were not more than twenty cattle to be sold. Of these, only two seemed worth bidding for – a beautiful little Ayrshire, newly calved, and another nice-looking beast which looked about two or three weeks from her time. There was a great scramble for the first one, most certainly the best animal in the ring. I muddled the business and lost her. When my second choice came on, I knew that I must secure her or return, after all that bother, empty-handed. I hung on, and got her. It was raining – cold, pitiless rain. When I had arranged for a truck, and bought hay, and paid for the cow, there was still a couple of hours to wait for my train. I was feverish, with a head like a turnip. Returning to the hotel, I dozed in the lounge till train-time. Asking the guard to push me out at Tyndrum, I relapsed into coma. On the high ground inland, another blizzard had started; the road was deep in snow and the walk to the warm, comfortable hotel, a mere 200 yards, seemed interminable. The poor cow, which had left Oban before me, must then have been shivering in her truck at Crianlarich, waiting to be attached to the morning goods train.

Long before daylight, I tore myself from the warm comfortable bed and plunged once more into the snow, with a rucksack and heavy case. There was no time-table at the hotel and no one was sure of the train. The road to the L.N.E.R. station was uphill and the dim light and deep snow made it difficult to follow. The bad going, the weight of the case, and the uncertainty of the time gave to that walk a quality of nightmare. I could see the station buildings far above me and when about half way towards them caught sight of the lighted windows of a passenger train. It could not be done, even had I the strength to hurry. Then I saw the train turn away, and realised that it was on the L.M.S. line. Picking up the case, I floundered on. When within hail of the station, I started to shout. The stationmaster came out, and asked, in unsympathetic tones, what I was shouting for, why I was walking where the snow was deepest, and why I had not taken the road under the bridge. To which I replied that I had never seen the place before, that I was ill, and would he please come down and help me. This he did; and finding that I was not crazy but in genuine distress, became quite friendly and set a chair for me by the fire, where I remained until the train came in.

At Lochailort, I found Graham and Maisie Bright. They were going down to Glenuig in the store-boat, and advised me to come with them and arrange for the cow to be met and housed at Inverailort, whence we could send someone to fetch her the following day. It was still very cold, with a fitful squally wind from the south-east. We cowered in the tiny cabin of the store-boat, praying for it to start. But unluckily for us, it was Ration Day; a lorry-load of boxes and sacks had to be stowed on board, as well as the various parts of a heavy marine engine. On reaching Roshven, Maisie and I were so cold that we decided to walk the rest of the way. Maisie had to push me up the hills, but the thought of a warm bed at Samalaman, from which I should not have to go out into the snow, sustained me to the end.

Two days later the cow arrived, led by the imperturbable Angus MacNeil. They had come in a deluge, even worse than the one Maisie and I had endured. Angus was soaked to the skin and had to empty the water from his Wellingtons. The cow was none the worse. We housed her in Maisie's byre and called her Maisie II. That night we had one of the worst thunder-storms I remember.

13

Amenities

As time went on and the issue of the war seemed no longer in doubt, the Crolls and I began to think of making ourselves more comfortable. For myself, the first improvement was a matter of sheer necessity. I have already spoken of the rusty steel sheets on the roof and of the bitumen paint with which I sought to protect them. At the end of six months, the rust was showing through two coats of paint; at the end of nine, the whole surface was riddled with minute holes. Clearly there would have to be a new roof – but of what? I wrote to the Department of Agriculture, politely suggesting that to send out roofing sheets without any kind of weatherproofing to people living in a wet, maritime climate was sheer waste of money, labour, and transport. They replied that my letter had been filed for reference: as for a new roof, they could offer neither slates, galvanised iron, nor asbestos tiles, but I could have sarking boards and roofing felt. They enclosed a specimen, of heavy quality and sanded. It did not look too bad. Reluctantly I sent an order; it might serve until I could get something better. In any case there was no choice. The steel sheets were finished, and it was rumoured that Jimmy the joiner would soon be called up.

The sarking boards arrived, with six rolls of felt and a note to say that the kind I had ordered was no longer to be had. The stuff they sent looked like tarred paper and tore as easily. Jimmy, aloft on a ladder, began to strip off the old sheets with a hideous clang. As they fell, I bore them away to a pile at the back of the garden. They needed handling with great care, so thin and ragged were they, and their edges cut like knives. Perhaps, I thought as I stacked them, they will be handy for something or other. I need not have bothered. A storm scattered them like a pack of cards; strewn among brambles and thorns, they soon fell apart and rusted away to nothing.

The house, apart from the cracked and gaping ceiling boards, stood open to the sky. We removed the bedding and small things to Annie's, while the less easily damageable pieces of furniture were piled in the middle of the floor and covered with a tarpaulin. Before the new roof was on there came a succession of pouring wet days, culminating in a heavy and unseasonable fall of snow. The satiny lining boards were streaked and stained with dirt and damp and there were four inches of water on the floor, in which the pile of furniture stood islanded. At last the weather cleared, the water drained away, and Jimmy resumed work. He had just finished the sarking and was thinking of laying the felt, when he received his calling-up papers. However, he said he would try to finish before leaving. Every man in the place and every ladder was mobilised. Some were below, unrolling the felt, measuring it, and cutting it into strips, others aloft on ladders, hammering home the tacks. No battens had been sent, and I was kept busy with a rip-saw, cutting every available piece of wood into narrow strips. At last it was done, and the trashy felt, unavoidably puckered and wrinkled, was secured with battens of every width and length. "It looks like a hen house", I thought, "but at least it will be watertight." To make sure, I gave the whole surface a coat of bitumen paint. The only thing that seriously worried me was that the battens were too far apart. If the wind got under that shoddy wrinkled felt, it would be the end.

Nor was I far wrong. Two months later, when I was spending the night at Samalaman, a gale arose; and on my return, in the morning, I saw that a big piece on the west side had been ripped away. It was Sunday; but when the neighbours returned from Mass, ladders were brought, and a new piece nailed on. I cut up boards I had been saving for other purposes and doubled the number of battens.

The felt was certainly less noisy than the steel and a shower of hail sounded more like peas than bullets. But it always seemed flimsy and insecure, as well as ugly, and after a time, I asked Angus MacNeil if it would not be possible to lay a thatch on top of it. He was not encouraging: the pitch of the roof was too steep, and the felt too slippery; the thatch would never stay in position. Then I suggested that we might stretch wires horizontally along the roof at 12-inch intervals, under which the rows of thatching could be securely jammed, and the usual sheep-netting above would keep the whole thing in place. He was still unconvinced, but offered to try. So I ordered one and a half tons of rye straw from a farm near Forres. Straw, I reflected, could not be adulterated; you got it as God made it. It makes a better thatch than rushes, and the rye straw is more durable than the wheaten. Needless to say, the worst thing was the transport. The straw was not baled, but tied into large bundles with a single band of twine, and proved bulky and awkward to handle. The first load lay for a long time at Samalaman pier, the sport of Graham's cattle. We had to wait for a dead calm, as the bulky and comparatively light stuff made a top-heavy cargo for a rowing boat. We were lucky in getting a light following wind, so that the bundles of straw acted as a sail. There was yet another load, which we persuaded the store-boys to bring in their own boat. They would not venture alongside the Smirisary pier for fear of the rocks, and who could blame them? They anchored in the offing and we rowed out to them and took off the straw.

The actual thatching took a week – six gloriously fine days in May, and I have never felt more exhausted. Angus MacNeil worked at top speed, while I pounded up and down the ladder, serving him with straw. At intervals, we stopped to measure and cut strips of sheep-netting, wishing to secure each section as completed. All this, when done every day for six days on end with a bare twenty minutes for dinner, was sore on the feet, the rungs of the ladder bruising the instep. But the result made everything worth while. The horizontal wires were all I had hoped; the sheep netting was drawn tightly over the neat layers of straw and weighted at intervals by stones hung on vertical wires that crossed the ridge. There was enough straw to make a thick thatch, which was pleasing to look at, warm in winter, cool in summer and, best of all, a refuge from the uproar of storms. When inside with closed windows, you could not tell if it were raining, or even hailing.

The same autumn, we thatched the barn on the shore with rushes. And Sandy Gillies, whose galvanised roof at the Goirtean was getting leaky, covered it with a rush thatch, using the same technique of wire. Hitherto I had acted only as assistant – by far the worst job. But the following year, when Angus Ruairidh was busy converting a derelict dwelling-house into a byre, he let me try my hand at laying the thatch and I made quite a good job of it. This work has, at the age of fifty-two, cured me of a lifelong fear of ladders.

In most parts of the Highlands, thatched houses were rapidly disappearing. But in Smirisary all the dwelling-houses but one, and all the byres but one, and all the barns without exception were thatched; and, what is more, in several cases thatch had replaced the ubiquitous galvanised iron. For this the war, with its scarcity of building material, was directly responsible; but many people began to see how much more comfortable, in a stormy climate, was the traditional roof, which could be made and repaired without cost by the people themselves.

None of my neighbours had any sanitary conveniences; but the remoteness of the place, the large amount of cover, and the extreme modesty of everyone made this want less vexatious than might be supposed. Living alone, I had thought nothing of it, but visitors presented a new problem. There was a little wood left over from the roof, for it is sound policy in the wilds always to order rather more of anything than you may need at the moment. So I began to build an earth closet. It stood in the angle of the byre and

118

garden wall, with a paved floor and approach, a thatched roof, and solid wooden walls and door. The seat was made of a wine-box in which I had brought my books; it still bore the inscription "This side up". Being in full view of the path, it needed an attractive setting, so I made a flower-bed beside it, which contained a syringa bush, a lupin, and a hollyhock, with borders of forget-me-nots and pansies.

Now that my house was more or less weather-tight, I decided to bring down some furniture from our old home in Ross-shire, which for some time had been let furnished but was now without tenants. These things would temper the austerity of my surroundings, keep me in touch with my traditions, and give me some incentive to good house-keeping. The transport was a risk, but one worth facing. I went up to Stromeferry, selected the things I wanted – a few good eighteenth-century mahogany pieces, with some rugs, books, pictures, and china – and sent the rest to a sale at Inverness. With the help of a joiner, I got the stuff reasonably well packed. Materials were scarce but we managed a crate for the big glass-fronted bookcase, and wooden battens for the bureau and chest of drawers. The chairs were sewn up in sacking. All this made a good lorry-load and travelled to Fort William by Cluanie and Invergarry, then by train to Lochailort, and down to Samalaman in the store-boat.

Here, as usual, we had long to wait for a calm day. The crate was too heavy to handle as it was, so we lifted out the bookcase, covered it with bags and laid it glass upwards in the bows of our rowing boat. The big cowhide armchair was securely jammed amidships and other things were stowed as best we could. Angus Ruairidh and Sandy were with me and whoever was not rowing took a spell of rest in the armchair. I wondered what the older generation, who believed in orderly professional removals, would have thought of this journey. At Smirisary we were met by the MacNeils, who helped to disembark the furniture and carry it up to the house. Angus MacNeil assured me that the bookcase was too tall to stand in the room. I had measured it carefully before packing, but doubt is infectious and I was on tenterhooks until it was levered into place with two inches to spare overhead.

I now had a neat, handy kitchen to work in, a comfortable little spare room for visitors, and a bed-sitting room for myself. I should have liked a bathroom, but that seemed out of the question and a weekly bath at the Big House did much to supply the want. The Chippendale furniture, hand-woven rugs, polished table, French etchings, Florentine and Breton china, shining brass and copper, and shelves of books gave me great pleasure whenever I came in from the croft or the byre. Contrast is the salt of life: I enjoy working on the land and also, on winter evenings, like to be surrounded by the apparatus of another world.

About the same time, the interior of the Big House was completely transformed. Mrs Croll, having sold her house in London, determined to bring to the Highlands its precious and beautiful contents. The next problem was what to do with the existing furniture, which had been included in the sale of Samalaman in 1942. Some of it was good, but more was ugly or shoddy, for the late proprietor had been more interested in letting the place than in living there. In the end, the larger pieces were sent to Fort William for sale, while the smaller odds and ends were sold by auction on the spot to raise funds for the new village hall. At last the furniture containers, which had come by rail from London to Mallaig, were brought down to Samalaman on a specially chartered boat. There emerged the most beautiful stuff – William and Mary walnut, antique mahogany, Persian carpets, pictures, china, books. Little by little the house was decorated to suit, the plumbing was overhauled and renovated and, last of all, the most exquisite plum-coloured and dove-grey plain pile carpets were laid in the bedrooms and on the stairs. I loved to walk barefoot upon them, letting my toes sink into the rich pile as into moss on the hill. There should have been a row of slippers at the front door, but the mistress of the house had no scruples about letting the rest of us walk about in tackety boots and Wellingtons. For village dances, the big Persian carpet in the drawing-room was rolled up and removed, leaving the polished boards.

In the summer of 1946, I suddenly found myself with a cook-housekeeper. I advertised the Goirtean house to let, with farm or domestic work available. There were over thirty applicants, but few of them wished to work and only one family proved willing to face a primitive cottage without a road. This was a disabled Merchant Service man and his plucky little wife, with three small children, the youngest a baby. Mrs Foster was a Glasgow woman, who knew nothing of animals or country ways; but not only did she clean my house and cook my food most efficiently, but was soon milking the cows, herding them on the hill, and catching and feeding the pony. Her husband looked after the children while she was at work, and did various odd jobs to help her and messages to help me.

The Fosters' arrival was one of those joint operations for which the Glenuig estate is famous. They were bringing their own bedding and dishes but I advised them not to burden themselves with furniture till they had been for a while in the place and tried it. So Mrs Croll and I collected between us a few simple necessities; we cleaned the house, arranged it, lighted fires, put flowers. Helen Bright and I, with two ponies, had previously taken down a quantity of coal. When the day came, we met the family with a horse and cart, and with Blossom, and with Hugh MacLean's donkey, and with a number of helpers, men and women: and the children, trunks, prams, cots and other paraphernalia were safely transported down the rocky, slippery path to the Goirtean. Blossom carried two rolled mattresses, and the MacLean donkey had a lot of parcels in one creel and the eldest Foster child in the other.

I hardly knew myself. Hitherto my household chores had kept me busy all the morning, and I could not get out to the croft or the garden till the afternoon. Now I could work outside in the morning and come in to an appetising dinner served in a well-swept, well-dusted room. The brasses shone, the silver gleamed, the mahogany reflected the light, the polished floor was almost too slippery. Cooking in a household with only one ration-book was not easy, but as long as the cows provided plenty of milk and butter we did not do so badly.

14

Fences and Drains

As soon as I heard that the Goirtean was to be mine, I knew that I must fence it. Low stone dykes and bushes thrust into gaps had met Sandy's need; for his house was in the midst of the arable and from the door you could see the nearer slopes of the hill grazing. Also he had sharp eyes and a good dog, and no sooner did the horns of a beast appear on the skyline than Queenie rushed out barking, and the raiders were seen no more. But from my house the Goirtean was hidden by an intervening knollie and I could neither see nor hear what was going on there. A fence I must have and it must be finished before the ground was closed for hay at the beginning of May.

At first I thought of employing a contractor, for long and bitter experience had given me a horror of amateur fencing. The contractor came and looked round; from his expression and manner I gathered that he did not think the job worth doing. In any case he could not undertake to have it finished till July. This of course was hopeless. The only chance was to get my own materials and persuade the MacNeil brothers to help me. Wire, barbed and plain, could be got without trouble by WAEC permit. The Inverness Committee was always very good to me; no request had ever been refused, and I had asked for many things – oilskins, alarm clocks, extra cow rations, Irish labour. I think they admired our enterprise, and the secretary, Mr Scott Swanston, was affectionately known among us as "Uncle Swannie". But stobs were to prove more difficult. I had a certain number left over from the previous year, when Sandy and I had fenced the north side of the Lon, but a good many more would be needed.

That first lot of stobs had not arrived without adventure.

They were landed from the store-boat at Samalaman pier during neap-tides. Now the arrival of goods is never officially notified and, if expecting anything, you must either walk the two miles to Glenuig pier on every boat day or else wait till someone who has seen your stuff lying somewhere remembers to tell you. And so it was not until a week later that I heard my stobs had been landed. There were seventy-five of them, and they cost 1s. 8d. each.

Riding down to the pier one day at a leisurely pace and enjoying the exquisite view of Rhu Arisaig and the misty Cuillin beyond, I saw far out to sea what looked like a long dark line bobbing and swaying in the swell. It was probably a mass of seaweed, yet had more the appearance of wreckage or driftwood. I was still watching it when a man came up the road and said: "Your stobs are all away – every one!" A week ago, they lay safely above high water mark but now a big spring tide had floated them off the pier and they were gone on some uncharted voyage. I looked again at the long swaying fine, and the truth dawned. "Are those the stobs?" I asked, pointing afar. "Must be", he agreed. I touched up Blossom and cantered down to the store. The boys were away in their boat, but their mother promised to send them in pursuit. That night they retrieved the whole seventy-five, half way across to the Arisaig shore. It was a marvellous piece of good fortune.

At that time there was a famine of stobs all over Scotland and there was no hope in the world of getting additional ones before the beginning of May. Droppers, however, were not so scarce, so we arranged to space the stobs at three yards, with a dropper between each pair, and to make up the remainder with birch posts cut in the Samalaman woods. I remember one parching day at the end of April, with a hot, dry, south-east wind, when I cut and trimmed thirty small birch trees at top speed, and carried them down to the road. It was a job I have no wish to repeat.

The work itself went with a will. The MacNeils did most of the hard labour, while I planned, contrived, and helped generally. Though strong and well-strained, it was not the kind of fence that would have pleased a contractor. We made use of rock faces, strong bushes and other natural things that would eke out the stobs, or carry us over a hard place in which no post could be driven. For on rocky, uneven ground orthodox fencing is difficult, even impossible, unless you use iron standards leaded in – a vastly expensive luxury. Our longest line of straight fence ended on the shore at Port nam Feannagan, where we were lucky in finding a jagged, upright rock on which the wires could be strained immovably.

The strength and speed of the men excited my admiration. We had no wire-puller, and they strained the wires – barbed as well as plain – with their bare hands and a crowbar. I myself did little but advise, discuss, hold things, collect what was needed, and hammer a few staples. Two gateways, seven feet wide to admit Blossom with creels, were left to enter, one near the house, and the other at the bottom to give access to the arable plot in the Lon Liath. The gates I made myself of poor, flimsy wood, the best I could get. They were the first swinging gates in Smirisary, and the old people, meeting in ghostly conclave on the sward of Cnoc an t-Sabhail, will shake their heads over such unorthodox novelties.

The Goirtean fence was finished just in time to keep the cattle from the growing hay. The next business was to enclose the stretch of rough grazing included in the Port and the Faing Mor. It would make a fine night park for the cows in summer and a place where Blossom could roam untethered. Not only might I claim the hill cattle subsidy, but should have a six months' respite from byre-mucking. The work was easily done, and required remarkably little material. On the west and north was the sea; on the south a stone dyke, which divided the Port from Angus Ruairidh's arable and needed only one wire above it. On the long eastern march, there was first the fence of the Blaran Boidheach and the garden and then a succession of low cliffs, which needed only a few short lengths of fence to connect them. The only difficulty lay in the hardness and rockiness of the ground. According to the contractor, nothing but iron standards would avail, but we managed without a single one. True, we had to drive the stobs where we could, regardless of symmetry, and use rocky pillars for strainers, thus sacrificing the straight line, but rarely was so large a piece of ground enclosed with so little labour and material.

The south-west corner of the Goirtean was very wet and so was the long gully extending from Cnoc an t-Sabhail to Port nam Feannagan. In former days, there had been a deep drain running from Sandy's old byre to the shore, which when periodically cleaned, kept all this dry. It now required a drastic widening and deepening and, as Graham intended to ask the Agricultural Executive Committee for a couple of Irish drainers, it occurred to me that I too might employ them for this work and also to make a reasonably dry and level pathway between my house and the Goirtean. Much of the old track ran over rocky steps and ledges, or on stepping stones through seas of mud – a trial to a walker and fearful for a laden horse. Formerly, when I had only scattered bits of land in the Goirtean, the pathway mattered less; but now, with myself and Mrs Foster continually running to and fro and the pony carrying loads of every description, it had become a necessity.

The Irishmen were to live in the Samalaman bothy and, as is usual, to provide and cook their own food. To my horror they were sent a week earlier than I expected and at only two days' notice. The bothy was ready, but there was no time to warn the Labour Organiser that the shop at Lochailort would not accept emergency cards, so that the men must bring with them bread, and all other provisions but potatoes and milk. And, as luck would have it, this was December, when milk was short and eggs as scarce as diamonds.

Early one morning they appeared at the gate with their

tools: an oldish man, John Doyle, and a boy of 20, Barney Callagher, both from the same part of Donegal. Like so many of their countrymen who cross the sea to labour in Britain, they were excellent workers. In less than a week the big drain and some smaller lateral ones were finished and running, with the cheery gurgle of liberated water. The ground, heavily water-logged by the rains of a wet autumn, was drying rapidly, and with the help of lime I hoped for a better crop of hay next year.

The path-making took longer, but it was a splendid path, with big stones below and gravel on top. We were lucky in having ruined buildings to plunder and a deposit of gravel in the brae above, which Barney excavated and barrowed where needed; where the distance was greater, we filled sacks and loaded them on Blossom. Doyle made a bridge over the big drain with flagstones quarried from an adjacent rock-face; planks he scorned. When still in Ireland, he had worked as foreman on the roads made by the County Councils to provide employment and give access to distant peat-bogs and thus understood to perfection the art of road-making in places such as ours.

The path was hardly finished when a new trouble threatened. Soon after the valuation of the Goirtean in May 1946, the unmortared wall of Sandy's barn on both sides of the door began to bulge dangerously outwards – so much so that several neighbours advised me not to put hay there in case the whole place collapsed. But I had nowhere else to store the Goirtean hay and the weather was too bad for outside stacking. So I decided to chance the barn's lasting through the winter: it could be repaired at leisure when empty in the spring. But by mid-December the bulge was visibly increasing, and, hearing that Doyle had built his own house in Donegal and knew all about dry-stone masonry, I asked him to look at the barn. He thought it might go at any moment. We went inside and, on shifting some of the hay, found that three of the solid oak rafters were full of dry-rot and had cracked, so that they sagged in the middle and let the weight of the roof thrust outward instead of downward, thus displacing the stones of the wall.

Doyle suggested cutting new rafters in the woods, also three or four stout props to support the roof while he and Barney demolished the listing section of the wall and rebuilt it with a little cement to give extra strength. The wood was cut and we were lucky to get a day calm enough to bring home the timber by boat. Somehow they jammed the new rafters alongside the broken ones and pulled down an avalanche of stones without burying themselves or letting the roof descend on their heads. But the whole thing looked so dangerous that I could not bear to watch them and was profoundly relieved when they appeared at dinner-time with the news that it was all safely done. The old door had fallen to bits in the summer but we made a new one from the stalls of Sandy's former byre, now used as a peat-store. We also deepened the byre drain, mended the stable floor, and laid some underground pipes in front of the house, with a trap into which dish-water could be emptied.

The Irishmen had been working with me for several days before I discovered (by close questioning, for they never complained) that the poor creatures were half-starved. There was something wrong with Barney's ration book, and both were living on Doyle's meagre provisions eked out with an occasional loaf of bread. Rationing is specially hard on workmen living far from home in bothies and doing for themselves, with neither the time nor the knowledge to contrive made-up dishes out of nothing, as the housewife is forced to do. For heavy outdoor workers, the meat and bacon allowance is fantastic. We all came to the rescue, as far as we could; one household would give a loaf, another some salt herring, a third a bit of margarine or a tin of baked beans. I bombarded the Labour Organiser with letters, wires, and 'phone messages, culminating in the telegram: "Irishmen without food. Please cope." This produced by return two large parcels of provisions. The men's gratitude was touching. "If it hadn't been for your kindness", Doyle said, "and for the kindness of other people, we would have to lie down with hunger." Drainage work in winter is no game for an empty stomach.

There was something very attractive about those two and they soon became an integral part of our community. Doyle was married, with a wife and small farm in Donegal. I often wondered that he did not tire of the homeless life in bothies and lodgings and labour camps; but as he said, he was a wanderer by nature and could not settle long in one place. He was a great teller of tales and his tin whistle was in demand at dances and at the games we had on Sunday evenings in the village hall.

15

The 'Star of Smirisary'

WHEN I first came to Smirisary, there were four boats in the Port, one to each household. Those of Angus Ruairidh and Alan MacIsaac were of the large heavy type in common use when fishing was a serious occupation; they were provided with mast and sail, which were now seldom used. Strong, steady, and made watertight with many coats of tar, these older boats were excellent for heavy loads and, for their size, not difficult to row. But on our rough, exposed shore, where it was dangerous to leave a boat at anchor even in summer, they were hard to pull up and required more men than the dwindling township could easily provide. Sandy Gillies and the MacNeils had twelve-foot dinghies, easily pulled and handy for an evening's fishing but rather light for large or awkward cargoes.

I had not been long in the place before I decided to buy a boat of my own. Angus Ruairidh, who had always been my sea-going partner, was thinking of selling his ark before it became unsaleable; and it seemed to me that a boat intermediate between the two types would suit us best – a boat light enough for three to pull up the shore and capacious enough to carry loads of coal and logs.

That was in 1944, when rowing boats were very scarce. I advertised for a fourteen-foot dinghy and answered the announcements of others, but nothing came of it. Then I heard that a Kirkwall boat-builder was asking for orders. Orkney boats had a reputation for sound workmanship at a reasonable price, so I wrote for particulars, put in my order, and a few weeks later the *Star of Smirisary* arrived – a strong beamy fourteen-foot dinghy, resplendent with white paint outside and green paint within. The only fault in her was the unseasoned wood of the oars, one of which, after a spell of hot sunshine, warped so abominably that it became un-usable. For long we carried it as a spare, but I was not sorry when a heavy log, accidentally thrown across it when un-loading, broke the wretched thing to bits.

Then, in an evil hour, I acquired with enormous diffi-culty an outboard engine. In my simplicity, I thought that it would enable me to go out alone, a thing impossible, on our treacherous coast, for a woman with oars only, except in very calm and settled weather. We could also, I supposed, go out when there was a contrary wind and, because of the increased speed be able to make two trips on one tide. But I was foolish thus to tempt Providence for no mechanical device has ever worked for me, or ever will. My oil-stove leaks, my clocks refuse to go, my lamp blacks its mantle, my electric torches are forever out of action. I have never driven a car because it would probably kill someone, nor owned a wireless set because it would cer-tainly drive me mad. Much as I loathe filling up forms and writing letters, tinkering with machinery seems to me an even more dismal waste of time.

The outboard came. There was staying at Samalaman an engineering friend of Graham's, called Ivan, who also owned one. He assembled the engine, fitted it to the *Star*, and accompanied me on its maiden voyage. At the eighth attempt it started with a splutter. Ivan remarked that it was a temperamental specimen but might settle down after a while. He was wrong. We wore out a number of starting cords; but never, while I was in the boat, would the engine even turn over, though it worked intermittently for other people. Every mechanically minded visitor at Samalaman spent hours tinkering with it. Finally I lent it to Donald MacLure, the shepherd, who induced it to work fairly well in another boat. The latest theory is that the propeller shaft is too long. Perhaps. But the fact remains that the engine will not work for me and, when I can summon up sufficient energy, I will sell it and with the proceeds buy a mast and sail for the *Star*. Angus was bitterly disappointed and others, no doubt, mildly contemptuous; but I must confess that I was not heartbroken. I hate the wretched thing, with its vibration and racket that drives peace from the sea and drowns its gracious noises.

The *Star* served us well, and under conditions that could hardly have been more difficult. We could go out only when there was a light breeze and little or no swell and must arrange to return at or around the time of high water. There might be weeks on end, especially in winter, when no boat could put to sea, and goods would accumulate at Samalaman, until at last they came down piecemeal on Blossom's back. Then, perversely, would come a long spell of calm, when there would be little or nothing to bring home.

In the calm frosty spells that come after the New Year, we would be busy transporting birch logs from the woods at Ardennachan, a promontory lying between Glenuig and Samalaman. This expedition would take a good three hours and could never be arranged until the last minute, owing to the uncertainty of the weather. When the flowing tide covered a certain rock off the Seann Rudha, I would look out from the house, and see Angus potter down to the shore and collect the oars and other things we needed. He would previously have secured one of the neighbours to help pull; and as soon as this helper arrived I would go down also. The pulling was the worst part of the whole thing. Pieces of plank, well smeared with wet seaweed, were laid at intervals under the keel, and the boat hauled to the length of the planks. These again were shifted forward, and so on till we reached the water.

Those days of frost had a beauty of their own, unsurpassed by anything seen in summer. Often the sea was like a mirror, reflecting the colour and shape of clouds; a smooth, glassy swell would rise and fall on the rocks, with a faint hissing and sighing. There was snow on the high hills, and rocks and promontories, especially in Muck and Ardnamurchan, were raised by refraction and seemed floating in the air. The low sun cast a ruddy light on everything, with deep purple shadows. A seal broke water, followed the boat awhile and sounded. Cormorants sat on rocks awash and now and again a heron flapped heavily shoreward. Off Rudha an Fhaing, a flotilla of eider duck were crooning. Miles away, on the Arisaig shore, a train could be heard labouring up the incline to Beasdale station.

Angus would take the stroke and I the bow oar, while Dileas, our sole passenger, lay curled on a sack in the stern. Sometimes we talked, for Angus dearly loved a crack and would often ask for a story. But somehow I never feel conversational at sea and there were long silences, until my companion in dreamy mood, would speculate on the origin of the swell that rocked the boat or on the movements of clouds drifting among the Cuillin.

As we rowed, the line of the shore, so familiar yet always new, opened up in sequence: the enclosure of the Faing Mor, with its jagged promontory called Rudha an Fhaing, and, about fifty yards off shore, the half-tide rock known as Boc Smirisairidh. This was a useful guide to us, for unless it were completely submerged, without broken water, there would not be sufficient depth to land at Smirisary pier. Then came the arable land of the Goirtean and the rough marshy Lon Liath, and, further on where the coast trended east, the green seclusion of Poll Beag, and Ardaniasgaich with its croft and safe sheltered little harbour. Beyond the Garbh-phort, with its shingly beach, we entered the strait between Samalaman Island and the mainland and, passing the boat-house, skirted the wooded shores of Ardennachan. Here, sheltered from the prevailing south-westerly winds, the trees grew down to the sea's edge – a striking contrast with bare storm-swept Smirisary. There was much birch, with a little larch, oak, and hazel. Half a century ago, there were no trees in Ardennachan and much of the ground was under cultivation. Then the Laird removed the crofters to the hill above Glenuig and planted trees to give cover for pheasants. The marks of the old drains could still be seen in the woods and on the abandoned rigs bracken grew shoulder high.

At last we reached an inlet where the rocks, flat and squared at the edge, made a perfect natural quay. Mooring the boat, we went up into the wood, where there awaited us a large pile of birch, cut on various occasions and left to be called for. This we carried down on our shoulders to the waiting *Star,* and then loaded, I handing the logs to Angus from the rock and he stowing them in the boat. The *Star* was now heavier to row, but her consequent steadiness made her more easily handled. If the tide were not too far in, there was no need to hurry; and we paddled along at our leisure, with a spell off Samalaman Island to let Angus light his pipe and hand me a morsel of chocolate. The familiar scenes were repeated in reverse; only there was always, even on the calmest day, a change as we rounded Rudha nam Iasgairean and met the swell of the never-resting Atlantic, fretting upon the rocks of the Lon Liath, with here and there a fang of broken water and a plaint that rose endlessly into the quiet sky. It was then that the Goirtean came into view and, as long as Sandy was there, we knew that he would see us and be down at the Port to help us unload. As we rounded the Seann Rudha and approached the pier, Angus would take both oars, whilst I, standing in the bows, would pilot him in.

Landing with a deeply laden boat was always a gamble. If the tide were unusually small or you arrived too early or too late, there might not be enough water and the approach to the pier was narrowed not only by rocks, but by large stones washed off it by the surf. At any moment a swell might rise, which would make the unloading, especially of coal, a troublesome business. Logs were not so bad, for they could be thrown ashore and, if they fell short, would float. Were the tide still flowing, we would pull the boat as far as we could by ourselves, stow the cargo somewhere out of reach of the sea and go in search of a second man to help us haul it home. If the ebb had begun and there was no one in sight, we left everything as it was until later in the day.

There was much pleasure in these home-comings but a

good deal of hard work as well. It was good to watch the little glen opening up, for Smirisary, like Glenuig, is best seen from the sea. Blue smoke rising from thatched houses, figures of men and women moving around them, the pony gazing at us from the Port, the cows winding down the brae: it was all very satisfying, and not least the sight of that pile of logs for the fire. But before we could call it a day, there was much labour in unloading the cargo and securing it, and then hauling the boat well above high water mark – sometimes, at spring tides or in threatened bad weather, right into the winter berth.

Firewood was our commonest cargo, but often we had coal, and sometimes provisions or feed for the animals. These last caused much anxiety, as they must be kept dry, and there was always a risk, not so much of taking a sea, as of a slip in landing, so unhandy was the pier. We always divided the sacks into half-hundredweight lots for ease in handling, whether we carried them up ourselves or brought Blossom down to the shore.

So far our boat journeys have been remarkably free from adventure. Angus maintained that the *Star* was a lucky boat, but he was always inclined to ascribe to luck what was due to design, for we never went out except in the best of weather. Once, however, we really were favoured by fortune. One calm and beautiful morning, on our way home from Ardennachan, we noticed the mysterious beginnings of a swell. As we skirted the Lon Liath, smooth green hills of water rolled towards us from the west; they passed under us and broke on the rocks with a dull roar. We had a large, mixed cargo and Angus remarked gloomily that we could never land, especially with a neap tide and but little water at the pier. Most likely we should have to go back to Ardaniasgaich, if not to Samalaman. However, we pulled on and, arriving off the Port, we lay on our oars and watched one swell after another climb the Seann Rudha and fall back with a low moaning roar. There was certainly very little water at the pier, and what there was drained out with each retiring wave. We were on the point of turning back when there came one of those curious lulls, lasting for a few minutes only, in which the swell seems to die away. Angus seized both oars and rushed the boat far up the shore. Delighted, we unloaded our cargo at leisure, for the ebb had begun. In the afternoon the swell increased greatly and no landing would have been possible.

Sometimes we were lucky in meeting Donald the shepherd, who went occasionally in the Crolls' launch to Eilean Coille, on which there were a few Shetland sheep. He would give us a tow to Smirisary, where we arrived long before we were expected. The only snag was the overpowering stink of the launch's exhaust, for we remained in the *Star* to cast her off at the right moment.

Usually there were all too few boat-days in each month; but the great frost of 1947, with its persistent easterly winds, gave us week after week of ideal sea-going weather. Tempted by the calm and stimulated by the cold, we brought load after load of wood from Ardennachan. Apart from this, the frost – for we had no snow – was an unmitigated curse. The burn was very low and frozen over, the pools and flushes on the hill were dry, and I had to water Brigid and Augusta at a pool where the ice must be broken for them twice daily. Not one fragment of ice could be left in, or they would refuse to drink. Worse still, Maisie the new cow, who calved at the end of January, had to remain in the byre day and night, and receive many large pails from the burn, warmed with kettles of boiling water from the house, for a cold drink would put off the milk. How I loathed those pails, especially in the early morning, when the ice was thickest. Once, in rage and impatience, I tried to break it with my foot; I succeeded, but the sharp edge made a neat cut across the instep of a sound pair of Wellingtons.

The frost brought its consolations. I had always wanted a porch to shelter me from the westerly gales and the Irishmen, whose drainage work for the Crolls was at a standstill, offered to build me one. They brought stones from the ruin

in the Blaran Boidheach and used for mortar the cement I
had bought for repairs at the Goirtean – our usual robbing
of Peter to pay Paul. The roof was thatched with rushes,
with sarking of slabwood from the Samalaman circular saw.
There were two windows, made from *cloche* glasses, and a
flagstone floor. I was immensely pleased with the porch: it
was six feet square, with walls eighteen inches thick and its
solid simplicity was in keeping with the rest of the house.
It cost the price of the labour and three bags of cement.
The men's rations were still coming very intermittently and
John Doyle remarked that they would be getting to Heaven
pretty quick with all the fasting they were doing. To which
I replied that there was no merit in compulsory fasting and
they would get to Heaven no quicker than anyone else. I
gave them what I could – potatoes mostly, and some of the
haggis that my butcher has sent me every week for nearly
seven years. With such a diet, there cannot now be much of
the Englishwoman left in me.

16

Birth and Death

AT the end of May 1947, we had our own version of the British heat-wave, with frequent plumps of rain, thunder, and murk. The hot south-easterly drift from the Continent met cooler airs from the Atlantic, breeding a low, stifling sea-mist, which lasted off and on for many days. The milk turned, the butter tasted like cheese and furry mould appeared on sausages. We were all tired and cross; the peats were not drying, and the potatoes were getting incredibly dirty. Weeds and slugs alone flourished.

For some days we had been waiting for Brigid to calve. I was not certain of the exact date of service; I had meant to write it down, like many another thing, and never did. Her rump muscles got slacker and slacker, her udder larger and larger, but nothing happened. Twice a day Angus Ruairidh, self-appointed midwife, came over to look at her: "Not today – perhaps not tonight. But soon – very soon." We did not want to put her to the hill, in case of accidents; and as she refused to stay alone on the comparatively level ground of the Port, the other cattle had to be with her – an annoyance, as Blossom was already down there, and I wanted to save the grass for night grazing later on.

At last the expert said she could not go beyond to-day. We let her out, but under close supervision, and in the afternoon we brought her into the byre. To pass the time, Angus and I sawed and split logs at the byre gable. We had not long to wait. Brigid, most placid and least troublesome of cows, calved quickly and without fuss. The calf was a large one, white, with roan markings, and a head very like that of its sire, Graham's Shorthorn bull. I examined it without much interest, expecting to find the usual male. But it was a heifer – the first I ever had in Smirisary. Heifers are as a rule quick to learn the art of taking milk from a pail, but Isabel – named after Mrs Foster at her own request – was unusually smart and at the second feed was drinking like an adult.

I was glad that the whole thing was over. The spring work, in spite of the Irishmen's help, had been strenuous and for some nights the dead, thunder-laden air had banished sleep. Those days of high humidity, with calms or an oven-breath from the south-east, the spongy horizons, the low dirty skies and rayless metallic sunsets, lay heavy on body and spirit. The previous night, there had been thunder in earnest; a storm, well out to sea, passed on a line from Tiree across to Canna and the south-western point of Skye. The thunder was hardly audible, a vibration rather than a sound, for the lightning, and most of the cloud, was below the horizon. From time to time, as if someone were swinging a lantern beyond the edge of the world, great sheets of light were flung into the sky, revealing the sharp, black peaks of Rhum and the hollows and convexities of distant clouds. Under that threat, the pale half-moon and stars that still floated dimly over Smirisary grew fainter, as if about to leave us for ever.

Next day, our world was dissolved in mist. The sea brimmed to the rocks without sound; as Sandy Gillies once put it, there was not enough movement to break an egg. A heavy stillness brooded over the world broken only, at five-minute intervals, by the fog signal at Ardnamurchan Point. Late in the evening, about eleven,* I went to the well for two pails of water. The mist was still thick, but there was sunlight beyond it and the glen had an aqueous translucent look, as if submerged by a sheet of clear and not very deep water. In the vivid young grass, starred with a million dewdrops, were drifts of bluebells and delicate cow-parsley and the rich glow of marsh marigolds, and the colour of these flowers, especially the bluebells, was so much intensified

* 11 p.m. Single Summer Time. In Smirisary we think in G.M.T. we keep S.S.T., and swear at D.S.T.

by twilight and moisture that it almost hurt the eyes to look at them. The well was full of that fragile mossy weed that looks bad in a kettle but does no harm at all. I was content, with that quiet, complete contentment that comes when the ragged ends are beginning to knit themselves up without, as it seems, any sensible effort of one's own.

The heifer calf had come as it were providentially to compensate me for a grievous loss. The reader will remember the luckless expedition to Oban and how Maisie the big Ayrshire cow came to us. That chain of misfortunes, it seemed, was not yet ended and some of my neighbours put it down to the slaying of her unwanted bull calf. After steering Maisie through the rigours of the frost and straining our resources to keep her supplied with suitable food, we lost her with summer in sight. For some weeks past she had been out with the others by day, readily adapting herself to a less pampered existence. Then one morning she refused her hay, and even her passionately loved dairy-cake, and her droppings were scanty and hard. Suspecting a bout of that common spring ailment, constipation, or "*tiorramachd*" as it is called in Gaelic, we kept her in and dosed her with treacle, but without effect. Then linseed oil was tried, and castor oil, and an enema, and even crude paraffin, but all without effect. She would eat nothing, and there was no relaxation of the bowels.

I felt pretty sure that she would die: you could read it in her sad, patient glance. No one who has once seen the strange withdrawn look in the eyes of a doomed beast can ever mistake it. And death, with the loss it entails, is not the end of a crofter's troubles. A new problem arises, more familiar to murderers than to honest men – how to dispose of the body; and a cow's body weighs about seven times a man's. In many parts of the country there are kennel-men who buy farm casualties to feed to their hounds; not so in the Highlands, where you must either bury the carcass or throw it into the sea. In rocky places like Smirisary, it is most difficult to find an accessible spot where the soil is deep enough to baffle prowling dogs. Many have had to sacrifice a precious piece of arable for this grim purpose. And if you choose sea-burial, it must be in a place where the body will not return with the next tide.

There is also the problem of how to get the cow to the grave. Thinking of all these things, it seemed to me that my byre, with its enclosing stone wall and long rough path to the shore, was a bad place for poor Maisie to die in. When Angus lost his red cow the previous year, it had taken six men to pull her down a short, gentle slope to the hole they had dug in the hay-ground. That was child's play to the job we should have if Maisie were left in the byre. And so, while she was still able to walk, we led her down to the barn on the shore, which at that time (April) was empty, for our remaining store of hay was in the Goirtean. Here we made a soft bed of old hay, and fixed a tying rope, and left her with sweet hay and tender tops of kale before her – none of which things she would touch. Twice a day we led her out to the water, and she would take a few sips; but drinking seemed to hurt her, and eating she never even attempted. Thus she continued for a week, gradually losing strength, until, early on the Sunday morning, I saw the beautiful head, so often turned to look at me, lying limp on the straw and I knew she was dead. I could have wept. She was a lovely cow, so quiet, so good to look at, and she had been with me only three months.

In the evening I collected the able-bodied men of Smirisary, and the two Irishmen, who were then draining at Samalaman. We surveyed the Port for a grave, but without much hope, for the turf lay on shingle, and the most promising places gave barely a foot to the spade. Our best plan would have been to drag the carcass to the sea's edge, and then launch the *Star* and tow it into deep water. But there was a stiff westerly wind and heavy swell, which showed no signs of abating; the easy way was closed and we stood irresolute at the barn door. Then Angus suggested that we might haul the body down to the shore and then somehow heave it into the sea from the Seann Rudha, whence it might drift clear of the Port altogether. We attached a stout rope to Maisie's horns and all together (there were seven of us) hauled her out of the barn and across the wet, uneven turf to the shore. She was a heavy cow, weighing perhaps 900 lb., and it took us all our strength to get her thus far: to drag her over the craggy, fissured surface of the Seann Rudha proved impossible. After some further talk the men departed and I was left beside the carcass trying to think of some new plan. For to leave her where she was – only fifty yards from the house – for more than a day or two was clearly impossible.

Then I remembered that Graham had once lost a heavy horse and could not remove it from the place where it died because the other horses refused to be yoked to their dead comrade. In the end, he tried the technique of crude and inexperienced murderers and carved up the carcass for disposal. Donald the shepherd was skilled in butcher's work; he was also interested in veterinary matters, and always keen to cut up any dead beast in the interests of science. I asked him if he would come down next day, dismember Maisie, and throw the fragments into the sea.

He came, with Barney as assistant. I begged him to excuse me, for, though also interested in science, I had been fond of the cow and did not want to see her drawn and quartered. So I went to hoe the garden and gave the men tea when they had finished. Whatever may have happened to the pieces, I never saw them. Donald reported that the cow was in beautiful condition, fat enough to kill, and nothing wrong with any organ, but the stomach and bowels were packed with undigested food. Later, the Laird was describing the case to his own vet., who said that the cow had been suffering from paralysis of the throat and hindquarters, and might possibly, but not very probably, have been cured by injections. This was a comfort, we could not have done more to save her.

I was glad that we had gone to such trouble to dispose of the body for, shortly afterwards, a heifer from another hold-

ing having calved at the edge of a cliff returned later to the
same spot and, being weak with the privations of a long winter,
slipped somehow and fell over. They found her later still alive
but so injured that she had to be shot. This carcass was dragged
to the shore, and then left, technically below the tide mark, and
far from houses. But in the warm weather, the place became
a social club for dogs, while people hurried by with averted
heads. I have not glossed over these gruesome details, because
they are part of our lives in the wild. When a beast dies, there is
the loss of money, the loss of a companion, and perhaps a blow
to your prestige as a successful farmer. These things are readily
realised. More difficult for the inexperienced to imagine, is
the amount of ingenuity and physical labour needed to tackle
the problems raised by 900 lb. of inedible beef.

Maisie died in April and Brigid was not due to calve
until the end of May, so that I and the four households
I supplied were without milk. Luckily they had a little to
spare at Samalaman. But I felt frustrated and dispossessed,
like one who had suddenly and as one thinks unjustly fall-
en into poverty. To have worked so hard and taken such
pains, and then to have no milk at all!

Then we heard that a neighbour, whose winter keep was
finished, wished to sell a newly calved cow. I knew the cow
well; she was old, and at the moment in very poor condition. But she had been a good milker in her day, and
there was nothing the matter with her that time and good
feeding would not cure. I bought three bales of rye-grass
hay from Samalaman to replace the last of my own in the
Goirtean which had been spoilt by an undetected leak in
the roof. We had been too busy repairing the bulging wall
in front and the worm-eaten rafters above it to notice a
hollow in the thatch at the back, which gathered the water
as in a basin, and let it seep through to the hay. The cow,
Julie, was small and stocky and brown, and had, it was said,
a dash of Jersey blood. Certainly her milk was rich, and
when the grass came, and Julie began to put on flesh, she
gave a fair pailful.

17

The Land Court Visits Smirisary

I HAVE spoken before of the incredibly small plots, some only a few yards across, into which our crofts were divided. This ancient system, called *runrig*, which in the eighteenth century prevailed all over the Highlands, still lingers in a few remote townships, though in a modified form: each man now keeps the same plots, whereas in the old days they were redistributed every year, so that everyone might get a fair share of the good and the bad. Of recent years, the demand for fenced and consolidated holdings has been spreading from the more progressive districts to the remoter ones, though in some of these it has not made much headway against the dead weight of conservatism and *laissez-faire*. But *runrig* is doomed, with many another picturesque and unpractical survival, if only because the ever-dwindling number of crofters makes herding and spade cultivation – you cannot plough or fence in *runrig* – an impossible luxury.

At Smirisary, the move for consolidation came, as might be expected, from the newest arrivals, Jean MacLean and myself, supported by the Crolls. We persuaded the rest to sign an application to the Land Court for apportionment, so that the patchwork of our holdings could be measured and re-distributed into continuous and easily fenced blocks of land.

So complicated is the law of crofting, so intricate the problems it has to solve, that it is necessary to have a body of experts to deal with these things. The Scottish Land Court includes not only lawyers and surveyors, but men well versed in human nature, with tact and understanding, first-hand knowledge of crofting conditions, and an ability to settle problems that would have baffled Solomon. There must also be a Gaelic-speaking member, for although very few crofters are without English, many can express themselves more easily in their mother-tongue.

The application had been lodged during the summer of 1946 and we all hoped that the redistribution would be done before the spring work of 1947. Winter or early spring, when there is no crop on the ground and the land can be seen in its nakedness, is clearly the best time for such an inspection, and high summer, when the crofts are smothered in long grass, tall corn, and bushy potato shaws, is quite the worst. Yet, owing to various unforeseen delays, the Land Court fixed their visit for Wednesday, July 2. There were three cases to hear: the redistribution of plots as between Jean MacLean and Angus Ruairidh; the exchange of the Blar Eorna, and some other plots I had adjacent to it, for a piece in the Lon Liath adjoining the Goirtean, which Sandy Gillies had always worked, though it was actually part of one of the crofts taken by MacAindreis, the tenant of Allt Ruadh; and a claim for compensation for a dwelling house.

As the day approached, Angus became more and more gloomy. An unusually wet spring and early summer had given a tall, lush growth of grass, and the tops of the rods that marked the boundaries of plots were barely visible. He remarked that if the Land Court tramped over every plot to measure it, the hay would be ruined, and anyhow the land had been divided like that for 200 years and should be left as it was.

Wednesday, July 2, proved to be one of those days on which a great many incompatible things happen at once; and just when the confusion becomes unbearable, a way opens, as if by magic, and the tangled skein unravels itself and all is peace once more. It was the time of spring tides, and the skipper of the puffer had chosen that very Wednesday to discharge our year's supply of coal. For the sake of those unacquainted with puffers, I had better describe the technique. The puffer is a small flat-bottomed freighter, built for transport to places where there is no pier. It comes in at the top of the spring tide, runs aground on a convenient beach and, when the ebb is sufficient, discharges its cargo into carts. The arrival of the puffer meant that every able-bodied man and any horse and cart in the place would be busy all day and part of the night, for the hours of the ebb were short and the skipper was bent on leaving with the morning tide. Some of the men required to unload coal were also needed at the Land Court session.

And, quite apart from the puffer, Samalaman was in a turmoil. As there was no hotel, the members of the Land Court had to be entertained at the Big House. The coal workers had to be sustained with food and tea. A bathroom was being put into the schoolhouse, and the plumbers, who slept in the bothy so long occupied by the Irishmen, had their breakfast and supper in the Samalaman kitchen. Graham was laid up with asthma, the cook and gardener were on holiday, Mrs Croll had a dreadful cold and, to crown all, had been urgently summoned to England to settle the affairs of a sick relative. Luckily for all concerned, she was persuaded to put off this trip for a few days. There was to be a session at the Big House at 11.30 to hear evidence, followed by lunch, after which the members of the Court were to visit Smirisary for the inspection of the land and the house.

At 11.15, I rode into the steading of Samalaman and saw a crowd of men waiting, with a strange horse they had borrowed to help with the carting. Some had come to attend the Court, others to shovel coal; you could distinguish them by their clothes. As I turned towards the house, Mrs Croll dashed out and asked me to go down with her to the pier, where the store-boat was expected to land our visitors. Descending the brae, we saw the puffer stranded. Her dark squat hull, scarlet funnel, and powerful derricks looked strange, bizarre even, but somehow pleasing in that setting of white shell-sand and clear unruffled water, with birchwoods in full leaf and, beyond them, the bare purple hills of Arisaig. The tide was ebbing fast but the water round the puffer was still too deep for work. A few more people were standing about, silent, as if wrapped in thought, and ready to stay there all day. As we picked our way over the slippery seaweed, the store-boat rounded the point and the Land Court party, with their cases and surveying instruments, were soon scrambling among rough and slimy stones.

The big drawing-room, so often used for dances, WRI meetings, and children's parties, had now become a court-room; the Persian carpets, beautiful antique furniture, and masses of flowers formed a strange background – intriguing too, like the grimy puffer in the still clear water – to our endless talk of boundaries and plots and compensation. The Land Court officials sat behind a William and Mary walnut table. Facing them, at a very respectful distance, sat a row of men, while the ladies occupied a sofa at the side.

The first case was the claim for compensation; the house in question was my own, which had lain empty for ten years before I took the croft and occupied the house. The reader will understand that a croft house, even if built by the crofter himself or at his own expense, remains the property of the landlord, who however must pay compensation for it when the croft changes hands. The same sum can be claimed from the incoming tenant. In this case, the claimant, a woman, had left Smirisary on the death of her parents and married in the South. Though she had never formally renounced her holding, no rent had been paid, no repairs done, and the land had gone out of cultivation. The difficulty was that neither the Land Court nor the claimant had seen the house as it was in 1942; its appearance in 1947 was naturally very different. The claimant, who was unable to leave London, was represented by her cousin and he and I had the difficult job of explaining the exact condition of house, byre, and land when I took over in 1942. We were both scrupulously truthful and thus our stories agreed; but even so there was a great deal of detail and the hearing took a long time.

Then came the matter of Jean's and Angus Ruairidh's boundaries. From the ladies' sofa, Jean put her case in English; then Angus came to the table, and gave his reply to the Gaelic-speaking member, who then translated it to the rest. He was a Lewisman and I had the opportunity of comparing the speech of Lewis with that of Moidart. When the matter of the boundaries, the peat-bank, and the method of measurement had been fully discussed, it was long past lunch-time, and my own case was quickly disposed of, for it contained but little detail. Also MacAindreis, for reasons best known to himself, failed to appear, and I am too fond of food to sacrifice a good lunch to talk, even about my own croft.

So after a few short exchanges we filed into the dining room. The lunch was as good as ever and the fragrant coffee put us all in a good temper. After a while we walked down to Smirisary. The Land Court were charmed with it. A misty drizzle hid the islands, but the air was sweet with thyme and wild rose and a soft wind brushed over the ripening hay, shaking the raindrops from a million heads. The senior member was an artist; I had seen some of his work in a croft house in Barra. While the others were dealing with Angus, I saw him making a few sketches from the top of the brae. First we examined my house and byre, and checked the details given before lunch. Then they went across to the crofts of Jean and Angus. It proved impossible to measure the plots individually without trampling on the standing grass, but bird's-eye views could be got from adjoining hillocks, from the various paths converging on the well, and from the edges of the potato rigs. Round and round they walked, five men and a woman, now in a cluster, now scattered, talking and writing in notebooks. I watched them from afar, not liking to go round with them, as the business was not mine. I was sorry that Alan Mac-Isaac, who knew more about boundaries than anyone in Smirisary, was at that time too crippled with rheumatism to get down the steep brae in front of his house. "It is a great day they are having", he said to me, as I passed near him on the way to the Lon.

Needless to say it was a matter of cattle that took me to the Lon in the midst of all this excitement. There is some kind of telepathy among beasts, which tells them when a gate is open somewhere or when their owners are too pre-occupied to give them much thought. On our way down from Samalaman, I had noticed that my cows were on the hill near the Lon fence and I was haunted by a feeling that they would take advantage of everyone being busy with the Land Court or coal-boat and get into some particular mischief. Leaving the party clustered on a hillock, I rushed up to the Lon, full of misgiving, though the place should have been safe enough for the MacNeils had fenced it the previous year. To my horror I found the barbed wire they used to close the entrance gap hanging slack, and Julie inside taking her fill of Angus MacNeil's corn. The heifer Rosemary was on the grass verge, and poor unenterprising Brigid outside the fence altogether. I harried them out, closed the gap, and drove them to another part of the hill. I seem to have spent much time running after Julie. Not long after this exploit, on a sweltering afternoon, when I had been thinning carrots and felt particularly bad-tempered, I spied Julie on the highest crag in our grazing, her stocky form outlined against the blackness of a rising storm-cloud. The thunder had changed from a rumble to a rattle: the ascent was very steep, and by the time I reached the cow, I was sweating, exhausted, and cursing. She seemed surprised to see me, though it was nearly milking time, and came down from her perch with exasperating slowness. The rattle diminished to a rumble and then ceased as the storm, with the inconsequence of its kind, by-passed Smirisary and rolled away in the direction of Ardnamurchan. Julie, chewing her cud in the byre, seemed to grin sardonically.

Returning to the crofts, I found the cluster on the hillock much as I had left it. It seemed, however, that they had agreed on a boundary pleasing to both parties, though the erection of boundary marks and the inspection of the peat bank must be left till next day.

Then we went over to the Lon Liath. It was beginning to rain – a fine penetrating drizzle – and as the ground was all in one piece, with the barn in one corner, the inspection did not take long. In the absence of MacAindreis, we took with us an impartial witness to look after his interests. Then we went up to the Blar Eorna, examined its rather complicated boundaries, and made a rough sketch map of the ground.

Next day, in mist and drizzle, the Court returned and spent much of the morning over the boundaries of Jean's and Angus's crofts. They were due back at Samalaman for lunch but as it was getting late, with no immediate prospect of the job being finished, I called them in to coffee. They were glad of it, for even in July one gets chilled by wading slowly in the rain through long wet grass.

The puffer lay at Samalaman for two days. The skipper was fuming to be gone; at the beginning of July there is no real darkness, and the men and horses worked through the night, thus making use of the midnight ebb. The ground near the boathouse was strewn with individual heaps of coal – two-and-a-half tons to each household. It looked a lot at the time but, as everyone said, it would not be long in going. But in lawful use, for in nothing is the honesty of small communities more evident than in their habit of leaving quite valuable things about, with the certainty that, as far as the natives are concerned, they will remain exactly where the owner had left them. "That coal wouldn't be lying there long in Glasgow", said one old man, eyeing the heaps. "No," replied another with equal cynicism, "nor in Fort William either!"

The puffer left on Friday morning's tide. Sitting at breakfast I watched her pass Smirisary, belching the customary black smoke. The squat, grimy hull receded till, off Ardnamurchan, it dropped below the horizon leaving, as its last farewell, a dark smudge in the air. As this dispersed the sea and sky became empty of life. I suddenly felt lonely and bereft. The ugly, dirty thing had been so long hoped for and its freight would mean so much to us in the coming months.

18

Haymaking

On a Highland croft of to-day, the chief crop is natural hay. This was not always so: there are people still living who remember the time when most of the arable land was under oats and barley, grown for human food and drink. Every glen with a swift-flowing burn had its mill and every township one or more whisky stills. But roads and railways, and the influx of cheap goods from the outside, put an end to this self-sufficing economy. Moreover, grain crops needed annual tillage and the declining population were no longer able or willing to face the labour, especially on the smaller crofts where the ground was turned with the spade. It seemed better and easier to grow potatoes for human food, to use imported oatmeal, and to leave the rest of the croft in grass for mowing. Natural grass, when carefully grazed and manured, will last indefinitely without turning, though in time it becomes dirty with perennial weeds and is less bulky than a short ley of seeds. But the variety of grasses and herbs it contains makes it more palatable to cattle.

Apart from a few rigs of potatoes, the Smirisary land was all in natural grass of good quality, except on plots formerly under potatoes, which had been allowed to go to grass. These were full of dockens and ragwort, which were laboriously picked out by hand at the time of mowing.

West Highland haymaking is a prolonged fight with the elements. The southern farmer, accustomed to speed and spells of fine weather, will never believe that any sane person could spend two or three months in saving three or four acres of hay. But when cutting is done with a scythe – and probably with only one scythe – when no more is cut than can be handled by one or two people – and handled very minutely and thoroughly, and when the air is nearly always too damp to do anything much till afternoon, it is a different matter. And it is worth remembering that in the Highland haymaking season – July, August, September – there may easily be six or eight inches of rain a month, making for the three months a total not less than the whole annual rainfall of Essex. When I came to Smirisary, I had already had sixteen years' experience of haymaking in the Highlands and was still undismayed, though now I should have to do my own scything.

The first swathes would fall about the third week in July, when the natural grasses were ripe and the red clover flowers beginning to fade. A faint tinge of bronze came over the waving surface, and people were busy at their doors setting and sharpening scythes, and looking over rakes for broken teeth. I myself had more preparations to make, for I was resolved to work with tripods, which at Fernaig we had used successfully in every kind of weather. This involved a couple of days in the woods, selecting and cutting between forty and fifty straight birch poles, and taking them home in the boat. However, I was not without help at any time. Several neighbours gave me a hand with the scything and, for three out of the four seasons, I had the assistance of various women students, whose keen interest made up for any lack of experience.

I do not propose to weary the reader with a description of the work of the first three seasons, but will pass on to the fourth, 1946, when I had the whole Goirtean as well as the Blaran Boidheach. The Lon I was forced to abandon: impossible to cart manure so far, and equally impossible – or shall we say inconvenient? – to house a cow there to make it on the spot. I had about twice as much to cut as previously but was well off for help. Mrs Foster relieved me of the cooking and housework, and the MacNeils came for an hour or two twice a week, and mowed enough to keep us busy for some time. Whatever additional scything was needed, I managed myself, with an occasional whetting by the experts for, in mowing, a razor-sharp blade is more than half the battle. Also for two whole months I had the help of a delightful Reading art student, Myfanwy Roberts, who spent her spare time in sketching our work and its background and who has illustrated this book. Having worked on her cousin's farm in Berkshire during the war, she could milk and do with skill many another farming job.

July was dismally wet and no one started cutting until the very end of the month. The MacNeils, always in the van of everything, were the first to begin, followed by Angus Ruairidh and myself, and then came the MacIsaacs and Jean MacLean. I always cut the Blaran Boidheach first; it was the earliest manured and, apart from an occasional visit from Blossom on her tether, was kept clear of stock all the winter. There was a thick standing crop, through which the newly whetted scythe, as yet unblunted by stones, swung with a rhythmic swish. The first day's mowing, like the earlier spring work, has that quality of eagerness and hope, unshadowed by later checks and disappointment, which is the crown of outdoor labour. But the Blaran Boidheach was not easy to cut; it was full of hummocks and hollows, of cairns and ruined walls, and you needed to know the ground very well to avoid spoiling the scythe, for under the forest of grasses all inequalities were hidden.

I brought out the tripod sticks and put them together. The sets we used at Fernaig were a modification of the orthodox sort and, I venture to think, an improvement. They had four legs instead of three, which gave stability in wind and made the coils more easily roped. The tripod method of drying hay saves all worry in wet weather, or indeed in any weather, for the grass is protected not only from rain, but from excessive bleaching by strong sunlight and, being entirely wind-dried, remains silky and green. For the sake of those who might like to try, there follows a brief description which others can skip.

The four poles, about eight feet long, are lashed together at the top and then splayed out to form a pyramid. A few turns of stack rope are wound round them to keep the grass from falling into the central space. The grass is then built up on the poles, until a hollow dome is formed, which here is called a coil. The part resting on the bottom of the poles is forked on top, so that the whole mass of grass is lifted clear of the ground, thus allowing a circulation of air underneath and inside the coil. Ropes are passed from leg to leg over the top for safety in wind. A well-built coil of this kind will ride out a gale and dry in the wettest weather.

Seeds hay, if the weather is reasonably dry, can be coiled on the day of cutting; but soft, lush, natural hay requires a day or two of turning on the ground. Our older neigh-bours, who were accustomed to the traditional method of spreading, turning, and building into small and then into larger solid coils, admired the tripods but did not copy them. There was the bother of cutting the poles, and they were always (to me irrationally) hoping for a "spell" which would make them superfluous.

Being short of tripods – there were only ten sets – I would, as soon as the coils became fairly dry, combine two or three into one, thus releasing poles for further use. And when I had a coil dry enough to take in – and it had to be very dry to pack in a closed stone barn – Blossom was brought and we made huge bundles of hard-pressed, tightly roped hay, hung them on the hooks of the pack-saddle, one on each side, and took them down to the barn on the shore. The poor beast looked like a walking haystack; but at that time of year, with plenty of growing grass before her, she made no attempt to eat her burden, as she did in winter, when carrying hay for the cows from the barn to the byre.

The closed barns of Smirisary caused me some worry. I missed the drying racks and slatted sheds of Fernaig and Achnadarroch; without their aid, the hay needed to be far more thoroughly dry when it went in. In so confined a space, you had to pack; and yet you could not pack too soon or too hard, for fear of overheating or mildew. So at first we piled up the hay loosely round the walls – and luckily in drystone buildings there are many chinks and holes – and later, when fully dried, we would fork it level and tramp it flat. As the pack got higher, two or three people were needed, one forking from below, and the others tramping above. Myfanwy and I would go over to Angus's barn and tramp for him, and he would come over to ours and fork for us.

The hay in the Blaran Boidheach took a long time to make, for the weather was unsettled and stormy, with one or two days of soaking continuous rain, when the level ground in the middle was full of standing pools. Had not our coils been raised from the ground their bottoms would have rotted. But at last we had them all saved in good order, and the tripods were folded up and loaded on Blossom for transport to the Goirtean. Here the conditions were perfect for scything – a wide open space, a gentle slope, without cairns of stones, without holes or rocks or ruins. Every few days the MacNeils came with their long sweeping scythes, and the swathes fell in orderly rows. Myfanwy and I followed spreading and raking; and the next day we built coils. The weather improved; we actually had a "spell" of three dry days in succession, with bright sunshine and a fresh northerly wind. The whole place burst into coils. Myfanwy, who must have made hundreds during her two months' stay, became obsessed with coils. She sketched them at all angles, and in every stage, from bare poles to the finished article, and to many she gave a quality of motion at high speed, making them spin like tops. In the Goirtean, they looked specially decorative, for their dull-green thimble-shaped masses were outlined against the blue sea and the faraway hills of Skye. The barn, beside the Goirtean dwelling-house, was near at hand and I found it simpler to carry in the hay on my own back, Myfanwy making the bundles and lifting them on to my shoulders. Sunday was often fine and the whole township, on its return from Mass, would be busy afield. To me, fresh from the rigours of Sabbatarian Lochalsh, this was a never-ending wonder and delight.

When the big flat of the Goirtean was finished, we mowed Glac Sloe an Lin – half an acre of sweet grass in a rock-circled hollow sloping to the sea at Port nam Feannagan. It was a lovely, secluded place, where the old people used to spread their nets for repair.

In September, we cut Glac Cnuic an t-Sabhail, and Port nam Feannagan. The upper end of this curious little glen was in good grass and easily worked, though the drier parts had been spoilt by rabbits and the long spring drought. But much of the lower end was damp and marshy, with sour and rather unpalatable herbage; and being surrounded on three sides by abrupt rocky slopes, it lost the sun too soon and was sheltered from drying breezes. The hay from all this ground we stored in the barn on the shore. Behind the barn was a cliff about fifty feet high and a few yards back from the top of the cliff was the boundary dyke of Glac an t-Sabhail. The easiest and shortest way to get the hay to the barn was to open a gap in the dyke, carry the bundles to the edge of the cliff, and throw them down, while someone waited below to receive them and pack them away. The last coils in Port nam Feannagan were bone dry and ready to come in, when a strong south-westerly wind sprang up which made the carrying of hay a toilsome and precarious business. We persuaded Angus to help and the three of us managed to get a dozen tightly roped bundles to within a few yards of the precipice. The wind was blowing inshore, coming in puffy gusts over the edge of the cliff. It would be dangerous to go too near with so top-heavy a burden, so we laid the bundles down and, waiting for a lull, pushed them over the edge with a rake, one after another. It was fine to see them hurtling through the air, with a cloud of loose wisps streaming from them, for the grass in Port nam Feannagan was very short. And that seemed a fitting end to the haymaking.

19

The Great August Drought

THE long frost of 1947 broke up in the middle of March, and was followed by a late, wet spring; at Strontian, near the head of Loch Sunart, over eight inches of rain fell in April. On the coast, we had rather less, but quite enough to make the spring work tedious and difficult. Never have I seen the arable land so dirty or found it so hard to clean. The ground was cold as well as wet, and every crop was late; early peas, sown in April under cloches, did not mature till July. Yet the air was mild, and we had no biting winds or night frosts to blast the fruit. May and June were muggy, moist, and sunless, and people began to worry about the peats. Weeds flourished abominably and the clearing and thinning of carrots, always a hateful job, became the week's cross. Peas, beans, and potato shaws reached twice their normal height. Luckily we had no gales to lay them; indeed, I never remember so windless a summer, with day after day of calm seas, when a girl could have taken the *Star of Smirisary* to Glenuig and back with a load of coal.

The hay crop promised to be very heavy, even on the newly acquired ground in the Lon Liath, which had been grazed with cattle until the middle of May. I looked at the lush, heavy grass, bending under its weight of water-drops, and wondered how in the world I was going to save it, supposing that we had a repetition of last year's harvest weather. Yet at the back of my mind was the conviction that August would be fine and I often said so to Angus, little knowing how true a prophet I would prove.

I cut the first swathe in the Blaran Boidheach on July 12 – as against July 30 in 1946. I was a week ahead of anyone else, and the experts said that the grass was hardly ripe. But having more to cut than they, and no man on the place to help, I did not heed them, and three days later the first of my student assistants, Peggy Lapham, arrived to give me a hand.

The mowing of so large an extent – for the new piece in the Lon Liath would add more than an acre to last year's total – was beginning to worry me. I was reasonably good with a scythe, but could not keep the blade razor-sharp, so that the work was heavier than it need have been, and could not be continued for very long at a time. In the Blaran Boidheach there were experts at hand to sharpen my scythe when needed; but in the Goirtean I was alone. So I used two scythes, and let Angus sharpen them both every morning and again after dinner; and by the time they were both blunt, I had done enough anyway. It was a good plan, but the carrying of two immensely sharp scythes backwards and forwards on that rocky path was rather formidable. The MacNeils came two or three times a week and, in less than an hour, they would mow as much as we could handle. They worked at high speed, cutting cleaner than a horse mower and very nearly as fast. I always left them the wide open spaces, where they could swing unhindered, and kept for my slower blade the bits and pieces and anything uneven, hummocky, or full of stones.

We spent an afternoon collecting the coil sticks from the arable plot, where, at the time of the deer scare, they had been used to support an upper layer of wire netting. To replace them, we cut three-foot hazel rods in the Allt Ruadh ravine and nailed them to the stobs of the original fence. I may add that I have never known a year when the coil sticks were not used for something else in winter, but so far I have always refused to cut them up for firewood, however great the need.

The Blaran Boidheach was finished on July 26. There were a few showers, but nothing to worry about: how different from the waterlogged misery of 1946! From that time until August 29, when the last coil from the Lon Liath went into the barn, we had not a drop of rain and hardly a cloud's shadow to make us look at the sky. As one blazing day succeeded another, we ceased to think of the weather, and the work became a monotonous sequence of cutting, spreading, turning, coiling, and carrying. I continued to use the tripods, because it was as quick as any other way, and there was always the chance of thunder; but as it turned out, the traditional solid coils would have served as well. Earlier in the summer, I had persuaded Angus to give the tripods a trial; and one fine day he, Peggy, and I rowed round to Ardennachan, cut six sets of sticks, and brought them home. But his conversion was ill-timed; he hardly needed to use them, and our conservative critics were justified.

In a sense the haymaking was easy, and never was the crop so quickly secured. But I shall always remember it as a monotonous grind, without interest or relief. The Laird, writing from Fernaig, complained that one might be working in a factory, with one day exactly like the last. Accustomed as we were to the fantastic fickleness of West Highland weather, with its sporting risks and frequent spells of rest, we became tired and irritable, and inclined to forget the value of hay secured without a drop of rain.

To me, the worst feature was the heat. The wind, nearly always from some easterly point, blew over superheated land, and often there was no wind at all; the sea was like glass, and the islands veiled in mist. Even the nights were stifling. There was a faint coolness in the early morning, when heavy dew saved much plant life. But by afternoon the heat of the sun was intolerable and, as its rays declined, the midges made life a burden. Under such conditions, scything became a misery. Though I wore nothing but an aertex shirt and thin cotton dungarees, I was continually bathed in sweat, and my clothes, full of grit and seeds from carrying hay and forking in the barn, stuck to my skin all day. And as luck would have it, the drought had spoilt the water supply at Samalaman, so that there were no baths.

After a while I tried mowing before breakfast. It was

cooler then and the dewy grass made easy cutting; but I found that extra work so early left me tired for the rest of the day and, after a week's trial, I abandoned it. I may add that anyone who wishes to slim in record time should try scything in a heat-wave. When it was all over, I found that my clothes were hanging in folds.

So little was rain expected, that we and everyone else would leave hay spread at night – a thing unheard of – without troubling to coil it, except as a protection from dew, and much of it went straight from the ground to the barn. Indeed, during the last week of August, some of the grass from the Lon Liath, where the soil was thin and gravelly, seemed almost too desiccated to be worth cutting, so that I was glad to have started a week before the rest. The only diversion was provided by a thundercloud, which appeared one day with dramatic suddenness in the north-east and rambled along the Arisaig shore to Mallaig, where, as we heard later, they had a deluge. We rushed to coil what we had on the ground, but we need not have bothered. Not even the fringes of that cloud reached Smirisary.

The unbroken heat was strange to us, and even stranger the long calm. The sea was like a sheet of metal, now dull, now shining, with hardly a ripple for days on end, and the shore uncannily silent; for the faint hiss and gurgle of the tide was borne away seaward by the prevailing land breezes. Now and again a mysterious swell would come out of nowhere, and set the skerries moaning, and we would watch the sky for signs of a depression from the Atlantic, and perhaps see *sgrioban* (scratchings), the fantastic whirls of cirrus that often herald a change. But the barograph marched on serenely, leaving a trace as straight as a Roman road, and nothing happened at all.

This weather was ideal for boat journeys; but as luck would have it there was little to carry, except some sheets of plasterboard for the Goirtean, which were too large for the *Star* to carry; the Crolls' launch was laid up with engine trouble.

After a while the seals and gulls got busy and we knew that the mackerel had come. Everyone with a boat was out, most of them provided with a number of hazel rods with feathered hooks, and a few with the "murderer", a metal shaft festooned with numerous hooks, which, when pulled up and down on a line, will catch hundreds in an unsporting but highly efficient way. The *Star* was out on several occasions, with one of us rowing, and the other two sitting on a plank laid across the stern, in charge of three or four rods. Sometimes fishing was combined with other business, and the silvery prey would leap and splash among paraffin cans and ration boxes. As fish always take better after sunset, we often came home very late, when there was only just enough light to see our way ashore. One night, when we had two women on board, neither of whom belonged to the place, the conversation had fallen on basking sharks, the mythical *each uisge* or water horse, and the Loch Ness Monster which had recently been seen once more by a number of people. As we skirted the rocks of the Lon Liath, I saw, in the still water among the skerries, a number of round, dark, moving objects, which I took to be the heads of seals swimming. Yet they were rather larger than seals' heads and it was odd that none of them sounded on the boat's approach. I pointed them out to Angus, who did not think they were seals: he was frankly puzzled. The two women were petrified, being sure, as they said afterwards, that these were the humps or coils of some marine monster. I was completely mystified, yet certain, in my matter-of-fact way, that there must be some quite ordinary explanation. As indeed there was. I heard voices and a moment later four young men in kayaks shot past us. Sitting in their tiny craft, they were so low in the water that nothing could be seen in the twilight but their dark moving heads. We never discovered who they were, whence they had come, or where they were going!

Towards the end of August, the shortage of water became acute. The Smirisary well, which had never failed in living memory, was still in action; but the water was clogged with filmy green weed and pails, when dipped, struck bottom. The well in the Goirtean, a shallower one, narrowly escaped running dry altogether and Mrs Foster had to be very economical, filling her pails with a cup and doing her washing at my house. We planned the making of a dam on the Allt Ruadh burn and I even wondered if September would see us carrying water from Loch na Bairness. But it never came to that. Our hill ground, with nothing but the smallest of burns and a few flushes and shallow pools, had become as dry as tinder, and the cows had to drink at the Allt Ruadh burn, nearly half a mile away. At night in the Port, they had nothing, for Tobar Mairearad was dry and not worth the labour of excavating. We had to lead Blossom twice daily to the Smirisary burn, itself a mere string of shallow, tepid pools. This was our third drought in fifteen months – May 1946, February 1947, and now August 1947. The West Highland country is certainly very wet, but in spells which, together, make up an imposing yearly total. Hill ground drains quickly and a month's drought can leave it very dry indeed.

The handling of milk became a worry, and butter-making a nightmare. The reader may remember that I, like every other crofter, possessed no dairy; the skimming pans stood on a table in the kitchen, which, as we never lived in it, was at most times reasonably cool. Some time previously, I had played with the idea of building a small outside dairy, but when I learned that in order to erect a shed six feet square I must submit plans to the County Council, I threw the official letter on the fire and did no more about it. Now I began to repent of my anti-bureaucratic prejudices. In order to secure sweet skim milk for calf and customers, I had to reduce the setting period from 24 to 12 hours, thus losing much cream; and whenever there was baking, I would shift the pans into the Irishmen's porch, with muslin cloths over them to keep out spiders and bits of plaster. This worked fairly well, except on thundery days when the milk under the cream would sometimes be as solid as junket.

As for the butter, it kept remarkably fresh; but the making of it was a misery, do what we would. We had the crock of cream standing in spring water, frequently changed; we cooled the churn with the same. We tried churning in the early morning, and churning late at night. We tried leaving the butter, when the buttermilk was drawn off, in the churn all night in a breezy place outside, so that it might harden before we washed and worked it. But it always remained too soft to work the water out and, in place of the neat patterned pats of which I was so proud, there were crude oily lumps which could not be sent by post. On August 17, the hottest day of all, I happened to be at Strontian, a warmer place than ours, visiting a local show of produce. The exhibits were in a marquee, in which the temperature must have been well over 90° Fahrenheit. A dairy expert was trying to judge butter in an advanced stage of liquefaction: I don't know how she did it.

Bringing the cows home from the hill, a job I had always found pleasant, now became a burden because they strayed so far, hid themselves so cunningly, and were never anxious to return. If you were very lucky, you might find them in ten minutes, or it might take an hour, for they were hardly ever in sight, and only an intimate knowledge of the ground, and of the grazing habits of our herd, as a group and as individuals, made it possible to find them quickly. On most evenings they were off my own hill ground altogether, in search of water at the Allt Ruadh burn, or of shelter from flies in MacAindreis's deserted byres, or browsing on the long grass by the bridge, or on the green foreshore of Poll Beag. It was Julie, for all her years a most active walker and climber, who led them on these distant expeditions. She was a boss cow, and having spent much of her life at Allt Ruadh, knew every hazel thicket, every ferny brake and rushy lair, every hollow among rocks, where she, with her small stature and brownish-red colouring, could lie undiscovered. Brigid and the heifers were more easily spotted, but until Julie was found there was no hope of turning home.

Sometimes I took with me one of the students and sometimes Mrs Foster's nine-year-old daughter. A small girl makes a fine companion on a cow-hunt; she can head off wanderers, round up stragglers and, what is more, worm her way through thickets too dense and skip over bogs too soft for stout and heavy-footed adults. We would climb the little hill above Faing Mhic Phail, and scan the horizon. Sometimes the cows were in sight, more often they were not. If they were not, we would try the derelict garden of Allt Ruadh, the big flat of the Laran Beag, the old byres, the green hollow by the bridge; and if all else failed, Poll Beag. To find them was one thing; to get them on the move quite another. Julie, if fiercely bawled at (her late owner had a hasty temper), would lead the way, usually in the wrong direction. But Brigid was a heavy cow, with tender feet that made her careful where she walked, and the two heifers were so replete that they moved like sleep-walkers, Augusta a long way behind the rest. Dileas, who could if she chose keep them going in a body at a brisk pace, would let out a few perfunctory barks and then fling herself on the ground panting, with an eloquent glance at me, as if to say, "That's that. Now *you* do something." The cows scattered and started grazing, and I knew that by this time Mrs Foster would have finished the dishes and be running out every five minutes to see if the procession were winding down the brae. I was very hot, even hotter than when scything after dinner, and the thought of sitting under a large cow bulging with grass, and radiating heat from a body whose normal temperature is 101° Fahrenheit, made me wish that I had no croft, or, if I had, that someone else worked it.

There were few evenings when the search for cows did not lead me across the waste land of Allt Ruadh, from which the tenants had flitted in the spring. They went out into the great world and its obliterating waters closed over their heads; we were left as we were, to watch the irresistible encroachment of the wild on the sown. Apart from the garden, the croft was unfenced, and a multitude of beasts – Graham's Highlanders, our own little herd, and three of the original stock left for summering – were knee-deep in grass that was formerly cut for hay. It was good to see the cows bulging with unexpected bounty, got without price or labour; but whether we love our neighbour or no, we must needs grieve to see his window blind and no plume of smoke in the twilight. A few months, even a few weeks, and what was once alive and working, however imperfectly, becomes in its dereliction an ugly thing, for the earlier stages of nature's reconquest are squalid and depressing. In Allt Ruadh you might study the first step towards the rushy desolation of the old crofts on the hill. Looking back from the ridge of Faing Mhic Phail, I could see the house, with the rush thatch – laid as at the Goirtean, on corrugated iron – slipping from the ridge, and Graham's horses sheltering in the lee of the porch; ploughed land gone back to dockens and sorrel; pitiful stumps of cabbage in a looted garden; trails of wire, a few pails lying about, a heap of unspread lime hardened to rock.

In the moist Highland climate, the invasion of the wild is almost as relentless, and the disintegration of man's works almost as rapid, as in the tropical jungle. Dockens and thistles, allowed to seed, spread everywhere, above all on turned ground which has been allowed to go out, for the original stirring of the soil causes countless seeds, lying dormant under the thick turf, to germinate and flourish inordinately. Rushes, when cutting and manuring cease, spread from isolated spears to serried clumps; brambles, unpruned, throw out invading suckers many feet long, which root ever farther afield until the whole place is covered with them. Fencing posts get rotten, lean, and finally break; wires slacken, staples fall, till we realise how much work, how much unending vigilance goes to the mere *upkeep* of a croft or farm. How easy it is to begin, how difficult to maintain; how delightful to build, how tedious to repair! It is the on and on that kills – the everlasting Monday morning or, for a farmer, the everlasting Monday and every other morning in the week. He that persevereth to the end, he shall be saved. Only he. A hard saying, but a true one.

There are different kinds of abandonment. Where people die, or get too old, with none to come after them; or where they weary and, after much neglect, throw in their hands and go. A serious defect in the otherwise excellent crofting laws is the virtual impossibility of putting a man out as long as he pays his rent. People are tempted to use the croft house as a home, while doing little or nothing with the land that goes with it; and this is the cause of much bad husbandry.

20

Autumn Days

AUTUMN might come in a sudden burst of storm, or summer turn to winter overnight. Leaves were whirled from the trees and the garden, still bright with flowers, was wrecked in an hour. There would be a rush to pull the boats into their winter berths, for a westerly gale, combined with the great tides of the equinox, might put the best secured things in danger of the sea. It was at such a time that three forty-gallon barrels of paraffin were washed off the pier at Samalaman and reported aground at the head of Loch nan Uamh, some miles to the north-east. Or summer might withdraw stealthily almost unnoticed, with little but the fading of heather, the reddening of bracken, and the haunting cry of migrating geese to mark the waning year. But always in storm or calm, we were deeply conscious of the ebbing of light from the world. As soon as the sun in its setting moved south of Muck, the pace quickened; soon there would be lanterns for the evening milking and a lamp on the table for breakfast. We began to notice the things that count in winter – the Aurora, the light of moon and stars, the winking flash from the lighthouse.

In every year there comes a moment – usually in August – when winter's shadow falls on us: an early intimation, not perceived with any bodily sense, for everything is as it was yesterday, but no less prophetically true. So in our inner lives there comes a day when we realise that henceforward, though there may still be growth and adventure, the general pattern will not alter. We can only repeat or, in kinder phrase, fulfil ourselves, for the end is implicit in all that went before. We have crossed a watershed and the streams no longer flow east to the promised land but west to the islands of the blest. To reach this point we need not be very old;

middle age, even early middle age, will bring us in sight of it. For the first time we see our lives not as a meaningless flux, but as a pattern, however ragged, a rhythm, however broken, of spiritual development in which our follies and failures, even our sins, fall into place. The missed opportunities were better missed; we no longer strive after the impossible, but accept our limitations and build on them. When youth departs, leaving us with most hopes disappointed and nearly all ambitions frustrated, it is easy to think that the rest of life is going to be uncommonly arid. But the desert has its own ways of blossoming and its fierce sun draws out the scent of aromatic thorn.

The year's round was finished. The last load of hay was in the barn, the corn-stack thatched, the peats in the shed. I was gathering fruit and vegetables from the garden, with no work but a little clearing up. There were potatoes still to lift but no one need hurry with these. The great labours of summer were over and the winter jobs – tending of cattle and mucking of byres, digging and draining – seemed still a long way off. The cows, sleek and fat with a summer's grazing, were still out at night and calves running loose on the green aftermath of the crofts. There was everywhere a relaxing of tension, a sense of completion and of leisure. The mornings were darker and we had no need to rise early. On Sundays, the faithful could enjoy the "long lie" of the urban infidel, for Father Bradley was away and there was Mass only once a month.

I began to enjoy receiving visitors. In summer, when every working moment was precious, I had, God forgive me, regarded them with weariness and distaste, as one might a visitation of flying ants. And it was in summer that they, like the flying ants, mostly came. Heads would appear on the skyline, gazing down upon the Goirtean and the Blaran Boidheach; and then strange figures would slither down the stony track, and every collie in Smirisary barked. I would straighten my back and look up, feeling suddenly rather dirty, tousled, and sweaty. "Damn," I would think, "I must pull myself together and talk intelligently." At Fernaig, when a car was heard approaching, the Laird would hide in the barn, leaving his wife to cope. But I had no one to cope and the place was bare and without bolt-holes. That was in summer. But in autumn the visitor is hailed with delight and I bitterly repent of my churlishness, and remember with sorrow the times I was chilly, monosyllabic, or brusquely rude; and the other times when, with greater subtlety, I suggested an interesting way home.

In September and October the herdsmen were busy. The cows were allowed on the aftermath for an hour or two only each day and this taste of green young grass made them unwilling to stay on the hill. They also had an insane passion for potato shaws and, if unattended, would make a bee line for the rigs, where their trampling did much damage. Angus Ruairidh spent much of his day watching his two cows. If he wanted to work away from the croft, or do any job that needed strict attention, he must shut them in the byre. Beside the burn, two representatives of the MacNeil-MacIsaac group patrolled ceaselessly. In most crofting townships, the whole of the arable is thrown open to grazing when the crop is lifted. But at Smirisary, each little group kept rigidly to its own ground and the unfenced boundaries must be watched with the greatest care. So restricted was the space available for each group of cattle, that it would have been difficult to do anything while herding, even had anyone wished to. Jean MacLean tried knitting, but the frequent interruptions were a trial. Reading would have been worse and meditation impossible. There was much desultory talk, but I often wondered what they found to say, doing always the same thing with the same people. On wet days, the sight of the old men standing hour after hour in their oilskins made me long to build them a sentry box with windows all round, like those set up in the streets of Punta Arenas to protect traffic policemen from the eternal wind of Patagonia.

The fence in the Goirtean did not solve all my own herding

problems. In 1947, the Irishmen had turned a specially dirty piece of ground near the Fosters' house and planted it with potatoes, which would not be ready to lift till mid-October. The plot was surrounded with luscious aftermath grass, which I wanted the cows to eat: yet they could not be left there for five minutes without a descent upon the withered and unattractive potato shaws. Not that these mattered but the trampling of drills knocked a good many tubers out of the ground, and, as Angus said, the cows might choke. So every morning we drove the beasts to the hill and over the pass, until the sight of the Allt Ruadh garden acted as a counter-attraction. In the afternoon, remembering the Goirtean, they would come home; and we would admit them to Paradise for an hour or two before milking-time. Here the Foster children kept watch and, if seen among the potatoes, the poor brutes were ruthlessly "hunted" away to Glac an t-Sabhail or Port nam Feannagan, often by Mrs Foster herself. I was once in time to see her, stick in hand, disappear completely in the Irishmen's drain and emerge a moment later, unhurt and laughing, to resume the chase.

We also had an uninvited guest. One night an old Black-faced ram of Graham's joined the cows on the hill, and came down with them to the Goirtean, where he took up his abode – it seemed for good, since neither sticks nor dogs would move him. He was steadily mowing down the best grass, so Angus MacIsaac and I caught him and led him back to Samalaman on a rope. Next morning he was back. For three weeks his woolly shape, curly horns, and indefatigable jaws were a feature of the place. Having recently listened to one of Boyce's pastoral songs, with words written in that classical jargon so dear to the eighteenth-century, we called him the Fleecy Care. At long last the shepherd removed him and he was seen no more.

There was now time to potter, even on occasion to dream; and always time to notice, with a pleasure that never staled, the many little details of my surroundings. There were the paths – not those consciously made, like the Irishmen's path, but the small tracks left by people's feet, widened and smoothed by use. When I first came, the paths were few, because my house had been so long deserted. The track to the well was faint, with grass hardly bruised; now it is a broad highway, worn and smooth. The path to Samalaman has become twice its original width. My cows, on their way to the Faing Mor at night, have worn a new track across the Port, in competition with a very old one made by Sandy's cattle and by heaven knows what previous generations. It is now crossed and blocked by a fence, but its surface is as good as ever and I use it for carting seaweed to Glac an t-Sabhail. Beyond the fence, just where the path skirts the precipice behind the barn, there is a rocky face worn hollow by countless hooves. In the Blaran Boidheach, which is crossed by an ancient right of way to Tigh Ruairidh, I tried, for the sake of conserving the grass, to make a new track, but it was a failure. You may widen a gap in a dyke or put up a gate: this, however much resented (for, in the case of a gate, opening and shutting is a bother) cannot be stopped. But it is easy to defeat the innovator who makes a new footpath: you merely don't take it.

Very few crofters carry seaweed nowadays; but the old seaweed paths, leading from the shore to the upper crofts, are still easy to trace and especially the flat green lawns, half way up the hill, where creels were emptied and their contents left for a time to dry and lighten. The constant fertilising of the grass has made it unusually green and fine and these patches will, I believe, be readily distinguished even after many centuries.

The hill is crossed by many peat paths; and even those leading to banks no longer in use are not hard to follow. They are full of associations and it is impossible to walk them without thinking of those who used them before us. For it was not with pickaxe and spade, but with the treading of feet, often under heavy burdens, that the hill-paths were made and maintained. The other day I was returning from Loch na Bairness to Smirisary and took Sandy's old path from his peat-bank high above the Loch and nearly two miles from his house. The bank is no longer used and the path less marked than of old; but I found the grass at the edge still worn and the stones smooth and rounded. How many times he travelled that same way, bowed under the heavy creel, and how many things he must have thought of on that solitary journey, day after day, especially at the rest-ing-places with which every peat path is provided, where the weight of the creel is eased against a rock, and the man stays to light his pipe.

The interval between the carrying of hay and corn and the lifting of the potatoes is traditionally given to thatch-ing. Rushes, which are now used in place of straw or heath-er, are then at their best, being neither too green and juicy nor yet withered and brittle with frost. We would cut them with a scythe – a tough job for which a special snatching stroke is required – and then bind them into sheaves and stack them till required. In 1946, Angus decided to con-vert an old dwelling-house near the shore into a new byre and I went to help him with the thatching. I began as the mere apprentice, running up and down the ladder with bundles of rushes, as I had done for Angus MacNeil in pre-vious years. But in the end I was promoted to do the actual thatching and did not acquit myself so badly. The worst part of this thatching business is the cutting and stretching of lengths of netting, and lacing them together with thin wire – a tiresome finicky job, especially on a cold day.

The following year, I had a much less pleasant piece of work. In May the barn in the Goirtean, so laboriously repaired by John and Barney, became too dangerous to use. Three more rafters gave way and the sag of the heavy roof caused a further section of the wall to collapse. I was worried at the time, for the date of the Land Court's visit had not yet been fixed and I was still uncertain if the barn in the Lon Liath would be awarded to me. Actually it was – an excellent barn, far superior to the other one, though rather a long way from the byre. But when the August drought broke, I found that the roof, which was covered with ancient and decaying felt repaired with rushes, was leaking in several places, and there was over two tons of first-class hay inside. I hastily ordered more felt and, while waiting for its uncertain arrival, patched up the worst places with additional thatching. It was a botched, make-shift job, done in too great a hurry and with too short a ladder. As a precaution I covered the main part of hay with a tarpaulin. I felt dejected. Twice, I thought, a barn has been valued by the Land Court and each time, soon after the payment of the valuation, something has happened to that barn. If ever I get another barn, I would rather it collapsed before the valuation.

Little by little the leaves floated down from the elder tree, leaving the clusters of berries in naked blackness. The heavy dark greens of late summer kindled to red in bent-grass and fern. Old scythes were made ready and we went out to cut bracken, partly for bedding the cattle but mainly to increase and economise manure. In many places bracken is easily cut, but not at Smirisary, where it grows patchily and always among rocks: for those who can use it, a sickle is better than a scythe. Also there were usually brambles among the fern, making it troublesome to lift. The other crofters stored their bracken in the natural caves which abounded near the shore and, when I first came, it was my grievance that I had no cave of my own, though this made a good excuse for leaving my litter uncut. By the Land Court award, however, I acquired a spacious cave in the Lon Liath. Like the barn, it was a long way from the byre and people warned me not to linger near the entrance, as pieces of rotten rock might fall on me. Judging from the fragments lying about, pieces had fallen, and not very long ago; but the cave was too good to miss.

Bracken I must have to eke out the manure. By May 1947, I had come to the end of Sandy's old midden and, as my cows lay outside for six months of the year, I should have a much smaller supply of dung than my neighbours, whose cattle were in at night all the year round. I kept Blossom stabled in summer, partly to prevent her from overeating but largely to conserve her droppings.

At intervals, when it was too wet for bracken-cutting, or potato-lifting, or too stormy for ploys in the boat, I would clear up in the garden, or work at a hundred odd repairs – rehanging and mending gates, tightening the wires of fences, replacing staples, building up gaps in dykes. The mere collecting of things that were lying about, themselves perishing and obstructing work, took far more time than anyone would think.

I also found time to get busy with a paint-pot. For a woman crofter, spring-cleaning is an impossibility: how can April, perhaps the busiest month of the year, be wasted on such trivial ploys? But in autumn, one might think of it and be content with a house that shines at Christmas instead of at Easter. The outside door and windows were badly needing renewal and the lobby, which had received only one coat in 1942, was desperately shabby. I had paint, brushes, even linseed oil; only the time, and perhaps the will, was lacking. Mrs Foster kept urging me to action, but I temporised; when this thing or that was done, I might consider it. But she, wise woman, persisted and at last, on a wet day, I made a beginning. The result pleased me so much that I willingly sacrificed a fine day to finish the job. The roof of the Irishmen's porch, owing to lack of proper material, had long since developed a leak. I had a roll of felt to lay under the thatch, but somehow it was always too windy to disturb the rushes, and I had become so used to putting a pail under the drip and removing the Wellingtons to the lobby that any other state of things was becoming unthinkable. I suppose it will get done some day – if we are alive, as Angus would say.

The potato shaws died down and the time for lifting approached. In 1947, we paid for our August sunshine with a wet and broken October. On a small croft, this mattered less, for working in twos or threes with a graip it was possible to lift a drill or two at a time and carry in the bags as we filled them. My real trouble was not lifting the crop but storing it. Smirisary swarms with rats and mice; there are very few cats, and the old ruins and deep drains give ideal shelter to vermin. In 1946, I bought a roll of half-inch netting and made a rough cage in the stable, but it failed for want of wood. The following year, with a much larger crop to protect, I was resolved at all costs to have a proper framework on which to stretch the netting. Some plasterboard; for the Goirtean house had arrived in a crate and the boards from this, together with a few odd bits of driftwood, were enough to make a frame about 9'x4'x3', complete with a lid to open. This, leaving some space for bracken packing, would hold about two tons. There is no worse job than working with netting that has been used before, and Angus and I spent a miserable day of rain in the semi-darkness of the Lon Liath barn, one hammering and the other holding a torch. The barn was three-quarters full of hay, which I had built into an L-shaped pack leaving a long empty rectangle to accommodate the cage. There was some loose hay on the floor, and we kept on losing our belongings – now the hammer, now the pliers, now my beret – and were looking for them with curses by the dim light of a 1947 torch.

There was an excellent crop in the new ground in the Goirtean – fine large healthy tubers, and very clean to lift. I was pleased, for the Irishmen had planted them in their own way and the local experts had been pretty sure they would not grow. Various members of the Foster family helped me and Blossom carried the bags to the barn, two cwt at a time.

Still days in autumn bring a special grace and the calm is enhanced by long hours of moonlight and the brimming, equinoctial tides. We know it is only a truce; yet each week as it passes brings us nearer to the return of the sun. A still sunny November, which often follows the gales and rain of early autumn, does much to put us past the weeks of darkness.

In 1945, the autumn leisure induced me to start a new venture, afterwards known as the Smirisary Academy. Maisie Bright's fifteen-year-old daughter, Helen, had just returned from boarding school in Edinburgh, where she drifted from one minor ailment to another; and having but little interest in learning and a great deal in animals and country life, it seemed a sensible plan for her to come home to Glenuig. To prevent complete barbarisation, I was asked to give her some coaching. The prospect was rather alarming. I had not taught for years, and never had I taken so young a pupil, or ventured on any subject but classics. I firmly refused to cope with preparing for any examination, or to have any dealings with mathematics, or with any science but agriculture. So it was arranged that she should come from ten to half-past twelve every morning and study English and history, geography, agriculture, and, by way of a modern language, Gaelic – for we both hated French. All this was not easy, for I had no help at the time and had to get my cows and housework done before Helen's arrival. She also, at the other end, had goats and poultry to attend to and usually rode down on her dun pony, with egg boxes and milk cans in addition to her books. We sat at the old gate-legged table in the window and never has schoolroom had a fairer view. Sometimes, in the middle of a Galsworthy play or a Gaelic exercise, some cow would break into the garden, or a pot would boil over, and there would be a rush to action. I taught her a little elementary meteorology and we would argue about the cloud-forms we saw in the great sweep of sky above the islands. Helen, who had been studying the Beaufort Scale, was longing to see a wind of Force 12, so that she might enter it on her weather record. But I, thinking of the thatch and the boats, had no desire for the spectacular. Force 2 was good enough for me.

21

The Highland Problem: A Few More Stones on the Cairn

IF any of my Highland friends have read with pleasure so far, I advise them to skip this chapter, for it may offend. The few things I have to say need saying and I shall try to disarm criticism by apologising beforehand for any corns I may tread on.

The Highland problem – what thing is not a problem nowadays? – has been endlessly discussed in the Scottish press and I can add nothing but a few observations, based on more than twenty years' work and residence in the West Highlands. By birth and upbringing an outsider, I am able to view things with detachment and yet, as a friend of Highlanders, with sympathy and understanding. Going quietly about my business, I am often supposed to notice nothing: and yet from an old fellow in Ross-shire – the "Jimmy" of "Highland Homespun" – I got an unsolicited testimonial, which I shall always value. "The bitch", he said once to the Laird, "seems half asleep, but she sees everything!"

I could if I liked write a great deal about the purely economic approach to human problems, which is one of the worst features of our dreary and servile age. But in a book like this it would be out of place and I could not guarantee to keep my temper. I have however tried to view the Highland problem from the personal and moral standpoint, while fully appreciating the economic proposals, as far as they go and in their proper place.

One might wonder why so many people take a passionate interest in the Highlands, in wealth and population so small a part of our country. Yet this is easily explained. There is the natural beauty, unequalled anywhere – a melancholy, nostalgic beauty that appeals to us in our disillusion, as it could not to the complacency of eighteenth-century enlightenment. There is the call of romance, of tradition – scorned in theory but still subtly seductive. And Britain, alone in Europe in her almost complete lack of a native peasantry, cherishes in the Highland crofter her only peasant survival. There is in most of us a hidden earthy streak, a love, almost unconscious, of little bits of land, that makes us idealise, in our undiscriminating fashion, the man with the croft. There is also the desire, frequently sincere but as often smug, to improve the condition of our less fortunate neighbours. Progress of the modern sort can be seen in Lochaber, at the industrial village of Kinlochleven, or in the new settlement (I had almost said D.P. camp) at Annat, near Corpach. But while praising these, what the Highland-loving public really wants is the lone shieling on the misty island, even if he would like to rebuild it in aluminium, or equip the island with "Fido".

These lovers of the Highlands, even when of Highland birth, rarely live in the land of their love. Gazing from a distance, they dream and theorise, or else, dwelling in cities where crowds are forever on the move, they are caught up in a whirl of economic and political planning and run here and there after this remedy or that, attending meetings, writing letters to the papers, reading reports. But the man on the spot, distrustful of theory as are most countrymen, does not talk much of these things. He grumbles vaguely at the government, because they are not giving him a new pier or a better road. But he rarely takes any practical steps to get what he wants by his own exertions, or to improve what he already has: this can be seen in many places and in many things, large and small. Away from home, away from the enervating and unpredictable climate, and away from the slow rhythm of traditional life, he would be different, just as his kinsmen overseas are different. And in the hard old days, under the spur of necessity, his fathers were different, for otherwise they could not have survived. If too little was given then, too much is given now – too much, and of the wrong sort in the wrong way. And it seems likely that emigration, whether overseas or to the towns, has drained the Highlands of the best and most enterprising, so that the home population, whether it likes it or no, can only breed from its weaker stock.

Meanwhile, no talk, no planning arrests the progress of depopulation which began after the potato famine a hundred years ago and gathered fresh momentum in the years that followed the first German war. In the earliest days, people went by compulsion, driven either by clearance or by sheer poverty. Later they went of their own will, because conditions seemed better elsewhere or merely because other people were doing it. For Dr Johnson was right in his famous phrase about the "epidemical fury of emigration". Human migration is infectious, it is in the air: where one goes another follows, as may be seen in any voluntary movement of population, like the Great Trek in South Africa. And in small isolated communities, where the need of able-bodied men is great in proportion to their numbers, if one or two families leave it will not be long before all are gone. It is in this way and for these reasons that small islands are evacuated.

What can be done? From the outside, very little. The State can indeed remove certain obstacles and disabilities, can iron out the irregularities that make the Highlands different – and who shall say worse? – than the rest of the country. It can stimulate and subsidise agriculture, industry, forestry, and fishing. It can provide transport, electricity and amusement. This sounds a great deal, and only a fool would deny its importance, but it fails to reach the heart of the problem. The State may do all this and more, but it cannot induce people to stay if they wish to go, nor make them willing to help themselves. Apart from the Outer Hebrides, where there is more virility, enterprise, and love of the soil, most of the young people all over the Highlands have lost interest in the land of their birth. Their future is elsewhere, their faces are turned to the cities or overseas. Many communities of the mainland coastal fringe are dead or dying, not of the isolation or neglect that catches every eye, but of the less obvious but far more deadly apathy and loss of nerve. Could the people produce a leader of their own blood and tradition, reared among themselves but with enough intelligence, drive, and vision to make them unite, there would be no more Highland Problem. But such a leader has not yet appeared and soon it will be too late.

One cannot read accounts of the Clearances without wondering at the meekness and fatalism with which people who loved their homes as few love them today, went to the coast, to the towns, to the emigrant ships, like sheep to the slaughter. True, their lairds had betrayed them, their ministers counselled submission, and the whole might of the law and the Kingdom seemed arrayed against them. Yet there was practically no individual violence, and certainly no leader to organise resistance – a thing which distinguished the agrarian troubles of Scotland from those across the Irish Sea.

To-day, the problem is far less arduous. Conditions of life are incomparably easier and public opinion has moved from hostility or indifference to a sympathy often verging on the sentimental. Yet the spirit is unchanged: there is the same barren individualism, the same mutual suspicion, the same waiting for someone else to do something. These are hard words and my friends and neighbours will receive them with indignation. Yet I am sure that many will agree with me, though they may not care to say so. It is time for us to strip off our make-believe and look into our hearts without pretence or reserve. Vanity and over-sensitiveness to criticism have ever been the weakness of the Celt, and few will deny that Stevenson's Alan Breck, with all his faults and charm, is a fair portrait of a Highlander. It is time that we ceased to regard ourselves as heroes suffering injustice and asked if our troubles were not due to some fault or failure in ourselves.

You will hear people say that the wet and stormy climate, the acid, stony soil, the remoteness and isolation can no longer be endured by modern people. What was once a challenge to resource has become a rock of offence, a thing that cannot or ought not to be faced. Yet all this was accepted with a merry heart by an older generation, who had not even such amenities as we enjoy. Old people, whose youth was full of discomfort, even hardship, have told me that they were far happier then than now. Perhaps the challenge was cheerfully met because there were fewer alternatives and because there were more people to share the burdens. Without State aid, men had to depend on themselves, to labour or starve; and thus the crofts were worked into a fertility we never see to-day when there are pensions and subsidies and grants for this and that but no corresponding hope or energy. The fullness of the old life, with its kindliness and gaiety, could come again, and come with new material aids, *if the will were there.* When they say that there is no work and no roads, this is only half the truth – and the half that matters less: indeed it is often no more than an excuse for rejecting the challenge. If the will were there, work would be forthcoming, and roads, for a democratic government dare not refuse to satisfy a sufficiently urgent and united demand. One of the greatest obstacles to Highland development is the doubt at the back of the public mind: Do people really want to be helped to stay? Or were it better to make some other use of the land? Roads, industries, electricity, amusements are all good, but secondary. The first thing is the courage that fears no work, the neighbourliness that is willing to co-operate, and a lasting love of the land and the things done in it. First things first: the rest will follow.

Whatever may be the choice and future of the Highland people, the challenge of the Highlands remains, and will never lack a response, though perhaps not from the race that once gave it. The glens will not be empty, but it may not be Gaels who fill them. A pity. But if they go, it will be of their own will. Those who come in their place will be men who can respond to an environment which, though always exacting, is never beyond a reasonable man's courage and resource. People are living, and will probably continue to live, in Iceland, in the Faroes, in northern Norway, under conditions far sterner than ours and there is more talk among them of settlement than of evacuation.

Of recent years, there has been a notable influx of outsiders, neither sportsmen nor sightseers, who have taken up land in the Highlands, often with succcess: people who wanted more scope, more freedom, more adventure than could be found at home. Naturally enough they have been criticised; and with justice, where they have ousted or competed with the Highlanders. But most of them took farms and crofts already abandoned and by bringing them into cultivation did no mean service to the land. Thus the drift from the country to town has been met by a more conscious, though of course less powerful, current in the opposite direction. This movement can only do good, however repugnant to the extremer type of nationalist, who sees in it a threat to Gaelic culture. But were Gaelic culture vital, it would absorb the alien minority, as it did in the Hebrides, even after 400 years of Norse domination.* Gaelic, receding for a thousand years, was doomed before any Lowland or Sassanach settlers came to the Highlands, doomed by the wilful neglect of its own people, even as the Gaulish language and culture perished, not by the sword, but from the passion of the Gauls themselves for all things Roman. This running after alien things – an old story, and a common one – among the Celts goes far to explain their failure as a race. If Gaelic (alas! for I love it dearly) were not in its last days there would be no need for societies like *an Comunn Gaedhealach*. The young people of the glens do not, and never will, draw their culture from Celtic antiquity; they get it from the radio and the newspapers. A few lairds and a great many hikers wear

---

* The only instance of the victory of a Celtic over a Teutonic language.

the kilt; but crofters and shepherds are clad in dungarees and ready-made suits. Not only is the big world outside so near and so strong, but the will to be different is weak or altogether lacking. The people want to go; or, if they are willing to stay, it must be under conditions which would make the Highlands no more than a well-run north-western province. As an individualist, and a convinced regionalist, I am more than sorry; but the fact is there, and we cannot ignore it. At long last, in spite of force or persuasion, individuals and nations get what they want, if only they want it enough. If Highlanders wanted a home in the Highlands even half as passionately as Jews desire a home in Palestine, they would get it in spite of every hindrance. But they do not want it enough and many of them seem not to want it at all.

The Highland problem is therefore at bottom moral, not economic. It concerns the human will and character and any planning that does not consider this is foredoomed. To make all things, even the highest, too easy, to hand out bribes and doles, to rob life of individuality, stimulus, and adventure is the fatal vice of democracy, and its viscous snail-trail winds all over the Highlands. Let us help people, by all means, but let us help them to help themselves. Men and women of the best type do not respond to appeals to our natural laziness and love of gain; they demand not tea and buns, but an opportunity for courage, vision, and sacrifice. When Churchill, in our country's darkest hour, offered us nothing but blood, sweat, and tears, he did more than make a phrase that will live in history: he read aright the temper of his countrymen. Now victory has come, and peace of a sort; there will not be much need of blood, and of tears no more than we are bound to shed as mortal men. But of sweat there must be a great deal if we are to have a sound and stable life in the glens.

22

The Amateur Crofter

HE who writes on practical matters, or about some special way of living, has rarely finished his job when the book is completed and seen through the press. There is always a crop of letters to answer – not mere fan-mail, but serious enquiries from people of all sorts who want to do likewise. These should be answered promptly and truthfully, and it is not always easy, for in most cases the honest reply is DON'T. Needless to say the enquirers are all educated people with other traditions: the sons and daughters of the croft, even if they have not sought a larger stage, have no need of advice, the knowledge is there already and what I have to say here does not concern them. I am speaking to people like myself; and because I enjoy my life, and am afraid of idealising it, I may have painted the shadows too dark and overstressed the discomforts, the intellectual loneliness, the lack of direct financial return. In order to be content with, and to make the most of, the kind of life described in this book, it is not enough to dislike the city, or to be tired of one's present job – not even enough to be keen on plants and animals, to be a lover of wild scenery, to be interested in practical farming. You must have a special temperament, which is a gift, and a special technique of living, which can, after much practice, be acquired. The keynote of this temperament is serenity and singleness of mind. The secret of the technique of living is to master your environment by yielding to it, to cross the stream by making use of the current.

For me, personally, conditions are ideal. I have experience, good health, equanimity, and a small private income which, as long as I am reasonably careful, saves me from money worries. I have no dependants whose just demands are a reproach: no near relatives to say: "My dear, how awful! *Must* you?" Without intending or even desiring it, I have reached a position where there are no personal claims to make or satisfy. No telegram can bring bad news, no letter anxiety or despair. These things are past and, at my age, can hardly come again. Personal ambition, never a strong motive with me, has burnt out and I have no children in whom or for whom it might be rekindled. There remain – and these, in the autumn of our days, should surely be enough – work, the fidelity it demands, the lasting satisfaction it gives and (to use a vague phrase for which the reader can supply his own content) the eternal values of the spirit.

Thus it is easy for me to work a small croft, and find my pleasure in it, and make a reasonable success of it. For most others it might not be so easy nor, even if it were, would it be desirable.

To take the young people first – for most of my correspondents are young – they may or may not have dependants or family responsibilities, but nearly all are without capital or private income and have their living to make. A Highland croft of the usual type and size – I am excluding the large holdings created by the Scottish Department of Agriculture for the maintenance of a family – will not provide even the most austere of livings without subsidiary work or private means in the shape of pension or unearned income. This point cannot be stressed too often. Such a croft will, however, provide a cheap home, a quantity of good food, and a few pounds beyond for other needs. It will also – and herein lies its chief merit – give a good and satisfying life.

There is another serious objection for the young, which will weigh not only with themselves, but even more with their parents. Crofting can lead to little beyond itself. There is not much opportunity of saving money or of gathering the kind of experience that would be useful on a large farm. An ambitious youngster soon reaches the point at which he sees no fresh worlds to conquer, and that, as far as the croft is concerned, is the end.

And few, till they have tried it, realise the monotony

of a life without evenings out, without week-ends, without regular holidays, without the relief and security of a weekly pay-envelope or monthly cheque. For the educated man or woman, the holiday question is probably the crux; but I am coming to that later. Apart from this, crofting offers little chance to expand, to make fresh personal contacts, even to find a mate. This is not to say that crofting is no life for a young person; but it must be a special type of young person – one who has, besides the capacity for faithful work, a varied store of inward resources on which he can draw in times of dearth as a camel in the desert draws on the reserves of its body.

And what about the middle-aged? They, it is true, often have the money; they perhaps have outlived ambition and the desire for crowds and change; they have achieved poise and equanimity – that is, provided that time has mellowed and matured and not merely shrivelled and warped their natures. They may have learned to demand less from their environment and to find more within themselves. But on a place like mine, the actual physical exertion may well be too much for them, unless they have been bred or trained to it. That is the snag for the middle-aged.

Now whether old or young, the amateur crofter must face certain hard facts. The ancient law – no cross no crown – holds good in every place, but perhaps more visibly here. And as Mrs Croll once wittily remarked of a neighbour we were wishing away: "Every Eden has its serpent." The reader of the foregoing chapters will have had this brought home to him; and if I have emphasised the cross, I have tried not to let its shadow hide the crown. If the enquirer, while reading this book, has been charmed by the inconsequence, the strangeness, even the absurdity of many of the things we do, he must realise what they imply, and think of them in terms of himself.

Work on a croft, though not insisting, as they do in factories, on the tyranny of the clock, demands regularity. Growth and the seasons wait for no man; if the potatoes are planted late, they will not come well; if weeds go unchecked beyond a certain point, they become ineradicable; if a cow misses the bull, farewell to milk when it is wanted. You may be ill, heart-broken, or obsessed by outside preoccupations – yet the farm jobs must be done as usual. Those of us who had children's ponies were taught to attend to our mounts before seeing to ourselves. This is sound doctrine and is instinctively followed by good farmers. On the lower level, such carefulness will save much money. On the higher one, it is part of that fidelity to vocation which you find in all those who love their work, whether they are doctors or teachers, shepherds or master mariners. They have that singleness of heart without which no work is truly well done and no worker thoroughly contented. As long as you are doing a thing, do it with all your might: if you cannot achieve this, give it up. A counsel of perfection, when we have livings to earn! But still it is worth keeping in mind.

I am not of course suggesting that anyone, and especially the educated, should not have other and various interests; the harmonising of these with the main purpose and the resulting intricate pattern, is part of the pleasure of living. Otherwise, we might become hard, dreary, single-track fanatics, even mono-maniacs, like the crofter Bjartur, the hero of that impressive but depressing Icelandic novel, *Independent People*. But the variations, however delightful, must not distract us from the main theme. Friends have scolded me, in the manner of friends, for having too high a standard of work. To which I would reply that my standard is no higher than that of any honest craftsman – though this, as one of the men remarked of Blossom's pack-saddle, "is getting rather obsolete". It does not really matter how high your standard is, provided you do not ask more from your subordinates than you are prepared to do yourself, or even as much.

It is in this singleness of mind, so far as the land is concerned, that the cranks are apt to fail, because they make the land a mere plank in some political or social platform. An individualistic country like Britain is bound to produce cranks and a small proportion of them in the lump acts not as leaven but as spice, which is good up to a point, but not in excess. They are becoming numerous in the Highlands, largely because the Highlands are a "problem" area, and where the problems are there are gathered the people with various and often fantastic solutions. Their presence may be, and usually is, stimulating and amusing *socially*; but if, in order to illustrate and advertise their theories, they take up land and try to work it, the result is not so good. Agriculture, that most stable and conservative of human occupations, must be done for its own sake and not for propaganda.

This is a book on crofting and I am too good a country-woman to bother my head about political theories. Those who love their country serve it better by making the best of the small fragment they personally control than by windy talk and the fanning of extinct resentment. Separatist nationalism is more than a political theory: it is one of the most poisonous of modern heresies, because at a time when the whole world is dying of hatred and selfishness it seeks not only to foment living animosities but to revive dead ones, or even to create them afresh. It is becoming more and more obvious, indeed it will be a truism to future historians, that the rise of aggressive nationalism in the sixteenth century was a major European tragedy, in which were sown the seeds of most of our present troubles. It is interesting to note that the countryman pays little heed to nationalist propaganda: it is a product of the towns, and appeals much more to an urban audience. The countryman will judge the nationalist less on what he says than on what he is and does in his own place. If he works his land well and is a good neighbour, that is fine; but then he won't have much time for propaganda. If nothing comes forth from the croft but floods of talk, the neighbours lose interest and finally respect. The Laird of Fernaig once criticised a schoolmaster who had taken up farming on the ground that he sat too long talking over meals. At the time I thought this an unjust criticism. I am not so sure about it now.

23

Conclusion

AND now I must gather up the loose ends and answer a few of the objections that people make to this way of living. To begin with, they want to know why I am wasting time, and the money spent on my education, in doing work for which no university training is required. The unequal yoking of authorship and farming, in which the farming gets by far the larger share, is a stumbling-block to many, though the combination of Martha and Mary in one person is not only possible but desirable. Poets have served their country in war, scholars have entered public life, and contemplatives like St Teresa or St Bernard of Clairvaux have proved the ablest of organisers. If this is true, what harm is there in the union of pens and ploughshares? The question arose only the other day, when the father of a boy told me that his son cared for nothing but poetry and was bitterly regretting his training for the Navy. With the eager single-mindedness of youth, he wished poetry to be all in all, not yet knowing that in this, as in everything else worth having, you must lose your life to find it. Charles Morgan, in his penetrating essay on Emily Bronte, stresses the value of humdrum everyday jobs as the "enablement of vision". It is in such discipline that the spirit finds its freedom.

I have mentioned already the need for the single mind in agriculture: in good writing the same thing is demanded. There seems to be a contradiction here; yet when we look more closely the paradox loses its sting. Perhaps I can make this clearer by putting aside generalities, and coming down to my own experience. I cannot remember the time when I did not want to write; and yet, when I gave up other work in order to devote myself entirely to literature, I had no success and at thirty abandoned the attempt, thinking that

I must have mistaken my vocation. Then I became a practical farmer: and it was only at the suggestion of a friend that I began to expand my farm diaries into the book that became "Highland Homespun" – a book which, to my utter astonishment, was accepted by the first publisher to whom it was offered.

While actually working on the book I gave it all my thought and could not have made it any better. But I was forced to write in winter only and at night, the work of the farm coming first; for long periods I would lay it aside altogether. But just as the marriages of sailors are notoriously successful, so dealings with the Muse may be happiest when she visits us, as Virgil puts it, shyly and at long intervals (*pudenter et raro*). These literary interludes are valued in proportion to their rarity. You cannot afford to wait for inspiration, or write only when you feel like it. In a crowded practical life, there is but little leisure – perhaps only on Sunday, or late at night, and you must get down to the job at once. At bottom, you want to write, perhaps above all things; and yet, when you take up the pen, you would rather do almost anything else. And so, in a few minutes, you must collect yourself and somehow create a favourable atmosphere, perhaps by reading something relevant, even if it is only the page you wrote last week. If the work in hand sticks, or will not come right, I lay it aside for some time, and often find later that the difficulties have vanished. It is possible that the work of the farm, especially on a little place like mine where there is not much worry or detail or personal friction, is favourable to such subconscious activity.

I have a strong feeling that if I gave up the croft I should soon abandon writing too. The two things seem not only interconnected but inseparable, like the two sides of a coin. The only complaint I make is that the croft demands so much of the *freshest* hours, so that when books and pens come out, they get no more than the flat tail-end, before fatigue drops down like a shutter. This does not so much concern writing, since you cannot even attempt to write when really tired. But often enough, when reading – and reading is, in the Smirisary life, a sheer necessity – the book slips from my hand, and I fall asleep with spectacles still on nose and lamp alight. And then the interruptions, with which the writer who lives another life is only too familiar; and beyond that the perpetual wakefulness bred by years of farming. Part of a farmer's mind is always chained to the sights and sounds outside. Yet the practical side of life has never come easy to me; and if I am now able – with not infrequent lapses into vacuity – to hold my own there, it is only by dint of constant effort. I am first cousin to that philosopher who, while contemplating the stars, fell into a well. Only here, I must be content to see them reflected in the still pool from which I draw water.

Then people say that a life like mine must involve much intellectual loneliness. This is a reasonable and serious objection. On a Highland croft, even if visited in summer, as you often are, by people who think your thoughts and speak your language, there are very long periods when there is nothing to break the sane but uninspiring rhythm of daily life. You can go away for a holiday – that is, if you can find someone to milk the cows – but the break is short, crowded, and full of preoccupations. Certainly the objection is valid and for many people insuperable; but for me there are countervailing things. If I were in a city, full of "interesting" people, I should only be a recluse. Shyness, never fully conquered, and the inability to express myself in conversation except with intimates, make the advantages of town fall rather flat. The only way is to accept this as one must accept any other disability.

Another common objection is that the man or woman who lives and works quietly in the country is an escapist. To this charge I would plead innocent, but if it can be proved against me, then I sin in good company. For what do they mean by escapism? Presumably the flight from an ordinary citizen's obligations and the pursuit of things which are of no obvious value to the community. It is a characteristically modern conception: whatever the contemporaries of Plato or of St John of the Cross may have thought of them, they did not taunt them with escapism. The idea, like the word, is the product of an age which values action above contemplation. In the religion of to-day, outside the Roman Church, the love of God, which once had the primacy, ranks far below the love of our neighbour, and religious people seem respected only in so far as they work for social reform and the promotion of a secular millennium. Except for the purpose of rationalising our desires and prejudices, we have not much use for philosophy either, and, in spite of our lip-service to natural science, we do not often think of it as the disinterested pursuit of knowledge, but mainly as a means to wealth, comfort, national aggrandisement, or even (like any other established orthodoxy) as an excuse for not troubling to think for ourselves. Hence if a person who might be doing social or political work is found writing books to please himself only, or indulging in idle speculation about the nature of things, he is an escapist, who should be directed into some occupation more profitable to the community. Very probably he has no social or political aptitudes, but only the making of a fine poet or scholar. Why not let him be? But of course if you deny the values you also deny the vocation.

It may be that even the most barefaced escapist can serve the community. There is a fashion for comparing our time with the dark ages that followed the disintegration of the Roman empire. Then, disgusted with a world that was not much nastier than ours, many of the best minds fled to deserts, to monasteries, to the small isles of the Atlantic and, in their flight, saved for posterity and for us all in the old Pagan order that was worth saving. The great European tradition, based on the double wisdom of classical antiquity and of Christianity, is now in hazard and it may need a new flight to preserve it for our children. Only on the physical plane there is no place of refuge left: no more empty continents or uninhabited territories in which, like the Pilgrim

Fathers or the men of the great Trek, we could live our own lives and think our own thoughts, free from the tyranny of governments and mass-produced ideologies. We can but stay where we are and look within ourselves for the only freedom which none can take from us.

From these matters, which I am not very competent to discuss, I turn with relief to something slighter and more personal. *They often ask: "Must you live alone? Don't you feel yourself getting queer?" No, I suppose I need not live alone; I could stay in a boarding-house or spinsters' hostel, for I have no near relations living, nor of my various friends are there any who would or could share my life. If I have not sought solitude deliberately, neither have I specially tried to avoid it: it has just come perhaps to enable me to cultivate certain talents that do not flourish in a crowd. In plant societies, there are some that need space and bareness for their development: the scattered, lowly flowers of the high hills could not live in the crowded competition of the jungle. So the mountainy or desert type of mind withers in multitude.

In the smallest community, there is no need to be lonely. Indeed, one's fellow-man may be near to oppression, as in lighthouses or in the camps of Polar explorers. The danger, I find, is not of seeing too few people, but of seeing the same people too often, so that an outstanding personality, especially if one dislikes him, swells visibly until he hides the sun.

Then comes that awkward question, don't you feel yourself getting queer? A question most difficult to answer, for all queerness is relative anyhow, and one's own queerness impossible to gauge. We are such stuff as dreams are made of, and your madness may easily be my sanity. This is ultimate; but one should not be perverse about it. What "they" mean, quite reasonably, is that without a comrade to be considered, we get eccentric and selfish. Undoubtedly

* "They" is here used, as in Lear's Nonsense Book, to describe the bystanders who watch one at work, and ask questions not always from pure love of knowledge.

we often do: but the constant comings and goings of the farm, the demands of neighbours, visitors, livestock, and crops break the self-centred circle and compel us to turn a sane face and offer a helping hand to the world around us.

The war, which brought me here, is over, and my early stringency is past. If I chose, I could sell up and go tomorrow, for nothing compels me to stay. But I do not choose. The work suits me, and no one still able in body and alert in mind can at this time take his hand from the plough. The day will come when I can no longer meet the demands of the wild; then I must seek a home with roads and sanitation and public conveyances. But not before it becomes inevitable. Often, from the hill behind the house, I look down on the croft I have built up, and wonder who will succeed me there, or whether, when I am gone, it will all revert to rushes. By crofting law, I cannot will it to anyone, because I have no relations near enough in blood; nor if I had, can I imagine any of them wanting to live on a croft in Smirisary. No doubt, in the fulness of time, someone will come; if not, I have done my best, and can do no more.

Last night, after a day of scything in the scorching heat,* I put the cows into the Faing Mor for the night and stayed with them awhile, as I often do, until the whiteness of Brigid was no more than a glimmer in the dusk. My head was haloed with midges, but being anointed with D.D.T. I saw them and no more. The cows, grunting with repletion, picked aimlessly at the rich grass and then lay down in a circle, one after another, their jaws revolving in a slow rhythm as they chewed the cud. Dileas, slimmed and exhausted with heat, lay stretched at length, like a skin rug thrown down on the ground.

The swell murmured among the skerries of the Lon Liath to the north and on the shingly little beaches of the Faing itself, without strength to roll the pebbles, and slowly rose and fell on the western verge, where the rocks dropped

* The abnormal heat and drought of August 1947 will long be remembered in the Highlands.

sheer into deep water. The sun had set, and the islands were shrouded in fog which had come in the van of a cooler air from the west. Far on the horizon, under a low arch of drifting vapour, was a narrow band of brightness with the visible forms of clouds, which widened until the whole misty arch rolled away eastward, and the glassy plains of the sea darkened under the coming breeze. It bowed the grasses among the stones, ruffled the dog's long coat, and then caressed my face, still damp with sweat and gritty with hayseed. I straightened my back, gathered my thoughts and turned homeward, with a backward look at the golden bar now fading into night, and the brightening flash of the lights on Eigg and Bo Fhaskadail.